Eleanor of Aquitaine

Heroine of the Middle Ages

MAKERS OF THE MIDDLE AGES AND RENAISSANCE

Eleanor of Aquitaine

Heroine of the Middle Ages

Rachel A. Koestler-Grack

CHELSEA HOUSE
PUBLISHERS

A Haights Cross Communications Company ®

Philadelphia

COVER: Eleanor of Aquitaine. Tombs of the Plantagenet Kings. Thirteenth-century abbey, Fontevrault, France.

CHELSEA HOUSE PUBLISHERS
VP, NEW PRODUCT DEVELOPMENT Sally Cheney
DIRECTOR OF PRODUCTION Kim Shinners
CREATIVE MANAGER Takeshi Takahashi
MANUFACTURING MANAGER Diann Grasse

Staff for Eleanor of Aquitaine
EXECUTIVE EDITOR Lee Marcott
EDITORIAL ASSISTANT Carla Greenberg
PRODUCTION EDITOR Noelle Nardone
COVER AND INTERIOR DESIGNER Keith Trego
LAYOUT 21st Century Publishing and Communications, Inc.

www.chelseahouse.com

First Printing

9 8 7 6 5 4 3 2 1

Library of Congress Cataloging-in-Publication Data

Koestler-Grack, Rachel A., 1973–
    Eleanor of Aquitaine: heroine of the Middle Ages/Rachel Koestler-Grack.
        p. cm.—(Makers of the Middle Ages and Renaissance)
    Includes bibliographical references and index.
    ISBN 0-7910-8633-X
    1. Eleanor, of Aquitaine, Queen, consort of Henry II, King of England,
1122?–1204—Juvenile literature. 2. Queens—Great Britain—Biography—
Juvenile literature. 3. Queens—France—Biography—Juvenile literature.
4. Great Britain—History—Henry II, 1154–1189—Biography—Juvenile literature.
5. France—History—Louis VII, 1137–1180—Biography—Juvenile literature.
6. Middle Ages—Juvenile literature. I. title. II. Series.
DA209.E6K64 2005
942.03'1'092–dc22

                                                    2005007489

CONTENTS

A Wedding That Changed the World

O n May 18, 1152, Eleanor of Aquitaine stood at the altar in a cold, stone cathedral in the city of Poitiers, in what is now France. The young man facing her at the wedding altar was Duke Henry of Normandy, Count of Anjou, the most promising young ruler in the land. The couple had a lot in common.

An unquenchable desire for power, seemingly limitless energy, and a strong will were just a few of their shared attributes. Few would have guessed that the wedding ceremony about to take place would change all of Europe.

Eleanor of Aquitaine was considered one of the most beautiful women of her century, but she possessed much more than long, auburn hair and a lovely face. Her intelligence, wit, and sophistication were unmatched by other women of her time. She cared little about what society expected of her and she carried herself with confidence and authority. Her free spirit and strong character—unusual traits for a woman of that time—made many people whisper about her when she walked by. Her previous marriage to King Louis VII of France had recently been annulled, ended according to the rules of the Catholic Church, but scandals and rumors about her marriage to the French king still seemed to follow her.

Now, Duke Henry of Normandy was about to marry Eleanor of Aquitaine, one of the greatest heiresses of the Middle Ages. Eleanor was Duchess of Aquitaine and Countess of Poitou, an enormous

Eleanor of Aquitaine was Duchess of Aquitaine and Countess of Poitou. Her beauty, intelligence, wit, and sophistication were unmatched by other women of her time.

Eleanor of Aquitaine was more than just a beautiful woman. Her wit and sophistication—traits uncommon to women of her time—helped her to outsmart many opponents throughout her lifetime.

area of the richest land in Europe. Duke Henry was already Count of Anjou and Duke of Normandy, and many believed he would soon rule the kingdom of England, as well. Together, Duke Henry and Duchess Eleanor would control the Angevin Empire, which included England and much of what is now France. The realm stretched from Scotland's border in the north to the Pyrenees Mountains on the southern border of France. At this time, the kingdom of France was made up of only Paris and the land surrounding it. The powerful Angevin Empire would, no doubt, be a deadly threat to the much smaller kingdom of France.

The wedding ceremony between Duchess Eleanor and Duke Henry was simple and quiet. By the time Eleanor's former husband, King Louis, found out about the marriage, it was too late for him to take action. The brief vows that the couple exchanged set into motion a sequence of politics and war that would last for the next 400 years, and the driving force behind it all was the masterful mind of Eleanor of Aquitaine—the duchess who outsmarted her most brilliant opponents.

Test Your Knowledge

1 Who had Eleanor of Aquitaine been married to before marrying Duke Henry of Normandy?
a. King Henry VIII
b. King Louis VII
c. King Louis VIII
d. King Henry V

2 What areas were included in the Angevin Empire?
a. England and much of what is now France
b. Spain and much of what is now France
c. Germany and much of what is now France
d. Italy and much of what is now France

3 Where are the Pyrenees Mountains located?
a. Scotland
b. Germany
c. France
d. England

4 At the time of Eleanor of Aquitaine's marriage, the kingdom of France was made up of
a. Paris.
b. Normandy.
c. Bordeaux.
d. Marseille.

5 Eleanor of Aquitaine's marriage to Duke Henry set off a sequence of politics and war for the next

a. 250 years.

b. 1,000 years.

c. 500 years.

d. 400 years.

ANSWERS: 1. b; 2. a; 3. c; 4. a; 5. d

A Young Duchess Marries a Prince

Eleanor of Aquitaine was born in 1122 in Poitiers, at the Castle of Belin, near present-day Bordeaux, France. Her parents were the future Duke of Aquitaine, William X, and his wife, Aénor of Châtellerault. Eleanor's grandfather, William IX, was the reigning Duke of Aquitaine.

At the time of Eleanor's birth, present-day France was divided into several kingdoms. Each kingdom was governed separately, often by people who spoke different languages. Aquitaine—at more than twice of the size of what was then the French kingdom—was one of the most coveted kingdoms in France. Aquitaine's lush land stretched from the Loire River to the north, to the border of Spain, and from the limestone hills of central France to the Atlantic Ocean. Many rivers and streams flowed through fertile valleys, rich with wild strawberries, raspberries, and cherries. Vineyards, olive groves, and wheat fields covered acres of land.

Although there was no unified government in Western Europe, most citizens did share one common thread—their Christian faith. Nearly all of the people in Western Europe were Catholic. The Christianity movement swelled, giving birth to Gothic cathedrals built to glorify God. People often embarked on long journeys called pilgrimages to pray at the feet of saintly statues. This strong Christian fervor inspired knights to unite as soldiers of God to fight in holy wars, known as the Crusades, against the Turkish Muslims to the south.

At the time of Eleanor of Aquitaine's birth, strong religious fervor inspired knights to unite as soldiers of God to fight in holy wars, known as the Crusades. Here, Cardinal Simon advocates a Crusade before Louis VII.

Eleanor was born into a feudal society. Feudalism—a societal system based on the idea that those in the lower classes could gain protection from those in the upper classes, in return for a kind of payment—

began in the Dark Ages. At that time, people feared attacks from those around them. There were the Huns to the east, the Muslims to the south, and the Viking pirates to the north. Faraway kings were too weak to defend their small kingdoms, so peasants often sought protection from the nearest armed knight. In return for protection, poor peasants promised to give local lords a share of their crops and other gifts.

By the 1100s, nearly everyone owed service to some else above them—peasant to baron, baron to count, count to duke, and duke to king. The king was the only person who did not pay service to anyone else. This did not always mean, however, that the king was the absolute ruler. Often, the man with the most land and the most peasants—or vassals—under him was more powerful than the king. Such was the case with Eleanor's grandfather, Duke William IX of Aquitaine. He owned more land and was more powerful than King Louis VI, better known as Louis the Fat.

GROWING UP WITH TROUBADOURS

From an early age, Eleanor was captivated by her

Under the feudal system, peasants often sought protection from the nearest armed knight. In return for protection, poor peasants promised to give local lords a share of their crops and other gifts. Harvesting and sheep shearing are shown here.

grandfather. He was the first known troubadour, a poet and musician who composed his own lyrics and sang them for entertainment. Unlike most writers of the time who composed in Latin, Duke William used French, the common language of the people. In this way, everyone could enjoy his songs. Eleanor loved to listen to the romantic love songs her grandfather wrote. To her, he represented the model gentleman and heroic knight—an ideal Eleanor would never forget. She was especially enchanted by the exciting story of her grandfather's elopement. According to the story, late one evening, Eleanor's grandmother escaped from her castle. She climbed onto William's horse, and the two of them galloped away into the night to marry. Much to Eleanor's sorrow, her grandfather died in 1127, when she was just five years old. Her father, Duke William X, became the new Duke of Aquitaine.

Eleanor's father was a powerful knight, known for his courage and valor, but he lacked her grandfather's charm and talent for poetry and songs. Still, he kept many troubadours in his court, and Eleanor spent many nights dancing to light music. Little is known about her mother, who died when Eleanor was only eight years old.

By age eight, Eleanor possessed the skills expected of a young lady of noble birth. She had already learned to sew, weave and embroider, and play the harp. Eleanor impressed her father with her skill at horseback riding. She could ride as well as any boy and preferred riding astride, rather than the more ladylike sidesaddle. Eleanor could also read and write—rare accomplishments for a girl during the Middle Ages.

Eleanor spent much time traveling with her father. It was during these travels that she learned the necessary skills for ruling a duchy, the territory ruled by a duke, such as her father. Once a year, Eleanor's entire household—family, knights, scribes, and servants—visited the kingdom estates. Her father collected shares of eggs, vegetables, chickens, and hogs. He also took home barrels of wine and sacks of flour, all gifts from the peasants. At each stop, his vassals would kneel down and pledge their loyalty to him. During her travels, Eleanor met all sorts of people—including beggars, poor peasants, merchants, wealthy ladies, bishops, and knights.

As Eleanor grew up, she won the love and respect of the people of Aquitaine. Her beauty and wit charmed many. By age 15, when her father died unexpectedly, Eleanor had blossomed into a spirited young lady. Her appearance was one of self-confidence. Thanks to her father, she knew far more about the world than most girls her age.

MARRYING A PRINCE

The duke's death brought an end to the long line of Duke Williams. Eleanor's older brother, William, had died as a child. The only remaining heirs were Eleanor and her younger sister, Petronilla. For the first time in over 200 years, Aquitaine was without a male heir. The entire land of Aquitaine would be ruled by 15-year-old Eleanor.

When King Louis received the news of Duke William's death, he too was dying. Though sick and sweating uncomfortably in the summer heat, word of Duke William's death brought some comfort to the king. As king, he could marry his vassal's daughter Duchess Eleanor to his son Prince Louis. In one swift move, he would secure the land of Aquitaine for the French crown.

King Louis knew he must act quickly. News of Duke William's death would certainly spread. It was quite possible that some powerful knight could kidnap Eleanor and claim Aquitaine for himself. Immediately, King Louis arranged for Prince Louis and a huge escort of knights to speed south, so the prince could take Eleanor as his bride.

Prince Louis was hardly the knight in shining armor that Eleanor had heard about in her grandfather's stories. Growing up, Prince Louis studied in a cathedral school, where he trained to be a monk. His father expected Louis's older brother to become king someday, but when Louis's older brother was killed in a riding accident, King Louis snatched the young prince out of the monastery. All of his years of religious training were difficult to erase. His quiet and timid manner made him an unlikely candidate for a knight and statesman. At the time of Duke William's death, Prince Louis was 16, only a year older than Eleanor, but far less educated in the ways of royalty. Eleanor expected, however, that she would someday marry a nobleman, who might very well be more interested in her empire than in her, and at least she was marrying a prince.

From a window in her castle tower, Eleanor watched the royal train ferry across the river. Wearing an extravagant gown, she prepared to meet her unknown prince. No doubt, the prince would be captivated by Eleanor's beauty. He would probably also be surprised by her confident and free-spirited manner.

Trumpets sounded and bells rang out as the wedding procession made its way through the cobblestone streets of Bordeaux. Houses along the wedding march route were richly decorated with banners and flowers. In a grand ceremony, the couple exchanged their wedding vows in the Church of St. Andrew. Tall taper candles lit the dark, stone interior, and the voices of choirboys echoed through the church. After the wedding, the couple was crowned as Duke and Duchess of Aquitaine.

Duchess Eleanor oversaw the wedding feast with ease and grace. She made certain that all of her guests had plenty to eat and drink. In between meal courses, entertainers performed songs and dances. The extravagant feast stretched from midmorning to late afternoon. Guests enjoyed lobsters, oysters, pork and venison roasts, platters of chicken and duck, vegetable pies, and breads. For dessert, guests chose from a variety of fruits, figs, and sweet tarts. During the meal, Eleanor noticed how shy and uncomfortable Louis acted. If he was really as timid as he seemed, perhaps Eleanor could mold him into the knightly man she had always hoped for.

After the wedding celebration, the couple set off for Paris. Along the way, they stopped in Poitiers, ancient capital of Poitou and Aquitaine's most important county. The Duke of Aquitaine was also the Count of Poitou. Therefore, Louis and Eleanor were also crowned Count and Countess of Poitou. The castle in Poitiers was Eleanor's favorite home. During their visit, Duchess Eleanor and Duke Louis stayed in the tower built by Eleanor's grandfather for his wife.

Eleanor's energy seemed endless. She arranged hunting parties during the day and entertainment, such as singing and dancing, at night. All of the celebrations were brought to a quick end, however, when the couple received some sad news. King Louis the Fat had died. The newly married couple, now known as King Louis VII and Queen Eleanor of France, headed north to Paris.

Test Your Knowledge

1 What was Eleanor's grandfather's title?

  a. Duke of Aquitaine

  b. Prince of Aquitaine

  c. King of Aquitaine

  d. Lord of Aquitaine

2 How much larger was Aquitaine than the French kingdom?

  a. More than three times its size

  b. Less than half its size

  c. More than twice its size

  d. A third of its size

3 Knights united as soldiers of God to fight in holy wars known as

  a. the Unification Wars.

  b. the Religious Wars.

  c. the Papal Wars.

  d. the Crusades.

4 The societal system based on the idea that those in the lower classes could gain protection from those in the upper classes, in return for a kind of payment, was known as

  a. monarchy.

  b. feudalism.

  c. socialism.

  d. democracy.

5   A troubadour was a(n)
   a. poet and musician.
   b. artist.
   c. court jester.
   d. skilled horseman.

ANSWERS: 1. a; 2. c; 3. d; 4. b; 5. a

Queen Eleanor of France

While Queen Eleanor may have been well prepared for life as an influential leader, she was unprepared for life in Paris when she and King Louis arrived in late August 1137. As the royal couple entered the gateway to the castle, Eleanor must have been uneasy about the dark, cold atmosphere of her new home. Louis

21

led his new bride up a long flight of stairs in the thick, stone tower that was to be her room. The only heat came from a few logs burning in an open fire, and a hazy smoke clung to the air. The narrow slits for windows allowed very little light to enter the room. The castle was dreary and dirty, much different than Eleanor's beloved home in Poitiers. The only lively spot was the courtyard garden, full of fruit trees and flowered vines.

Beyond the castle walls, the streets were noisy and crowded. Merchants yelled out prices of breads and pastries. Goats and pigs roamed along the dirt roads. The women were timid and proper, and their clothing lacked style and flair. The men seemed much more serious than Eleanor's light-hearted Aquitainians.

Queen Eleanor had the power to change her surroundings—and change them she did. She ordered colorful tapestries to hang on the walls. She hired workers to build a fireplace with a chimney. She had the narrow windows widened and shutters added. She put the servants under strict management and required them to wash their hands before serving meals.

Eleanor's mother-in-law, widowed Queen Adelaide, immediately disliked her. Perhaps she thought her religious son was too good for the easy-mannered duchess. Queen Adelaide disapproved of Eleanor's lavish spending on fancy decorations, silk dresses, and noisy entertainment. The group of southern friends that Eleanor brought with her—troubadours, knights, and outspoken ladies—was too much for her mother-in-law to take. Not long after Eleanor arrived at the castle, Queen Adelaide moved out, to a more quiet country estate.

Although Queen Eleanor had triumphed over her mother-in-law, she had less success with her husband, who was not transforming into the dashing knight she had hoped he would become. King Louis spent most of his time praying, rather than tending to his kingly duties. At least he did not object to Eleanor's spending habits and festivities. In fact, he was captivated by her beauty and desperately wanted to win her love. One of the king's friends commented, "He loved the Queen almost beyond reason." [1] This love caused King Louis to make some hasty decisions, however.

In order to prove to Eleanor that he was a strong king, Louis sometimes masked his shyness by going to extremes. Late in 1137, the couple got news of a revolt in Eleanor's favorite city of Poitiers. King Louis and his armed knights hurried south with amazing speed. He would show his queen how swiftly he could deal with these rebels. The group

A Woman Before Her Time

Eleanor of Aquitaine lived during the Middle Ages, the period between the fall of Rome, in the year 476, and the start of the Renaissance some 1,000 years later. She was considered by many to have been a woman before her time. She accomplished things that women of her time did not even dare to imagine.

Despite the fact that she lived hundreds of years before the historical period of rebirth known as the Renaissance, Eleanor of Aquitaine re-created herself many times over. The word *renaissance* comes from the Latin word *renasci*, meaning "reborn." Beginning in Italy in the 1400s, and lasting over the next several centuries, the Renaissance spread throughout Europe. The period finally ended around 1600. The Renaissance marked a rebirth in caught the rebels off guard and easily stomped out the rebellion, but King Louis did not stop with a simple victory. He unleashed harsh punishments on all of the townspeople. He then chopped off the hands of each rebel leader. In Paris, Queen Eleanor did not take well to the news of her husband's brutal behavior. The king was supposed to be a

learning and in the arts of ancient Greece and Rome. It marked a revival of classical wisdom and beauty. The Renaissance was also a time of discovery and exploration.

Through newly discovered trade routes, Europeans were exposed to fresh ideas and new possibilities. People began to ask questions about life and searched to uncover the answers. Artists became fascinated with the human body and tried to create pictures and sculptures as lifelike and realistic as possible. The Renaissance was an exciting era for Europeans. Much like those born during the Renaissance, Eleanor of Aquitaine, a woman before her time, pushed the boundaries of her role as a woman in the Middle Ages.

In a show of his love for Eleanor, King Louis tried to put down a revolt in Eleanor's favorite city of Poitiers. King Louis and his armed knights hurried south with amazing speed.

fearless knight, not a horrible tyrant. Above all, King Louis needed to be the kind of king that both Queen Eleanor and her people could respect.

TRAGEDY AT VITRY

Five years later, in January 1143, King Louis again let his rash behavior get the best of him. This time, his decision left a sting that he would never forget. King Louis had a disagreement with one of his vassals—the Count of Champagne—about who would be archbishop of the church there. The count wanted to keep the archbishop who had already been appointed by the church. King Louis stubbornly insisted on his own choice. The pope had to step in to resolve the argument. In a letter, the pope told King Louis that the current archbishop would stay. Embarrassed by the pope's rebuke, King Louis became more stubborn than ever. Finally, the pope was forced to excommunicate King Louis, meaning he lost his membership privileges in the Catholic Church.

Eleanor's father and grandfather had both been excommunicated several times. They simply chose to ignore the punishment, but with his religious background, King Louis handled the situation differently. In view of his devotion to God, excommunication was unbearable. He decided to take matters into his own hands.

King Louis blamed the Count of Champagne for all of his troubles. He called together an army of knights and invaded Champagne. His knights attacked the town of Vitry and took the townspeople by surprise. During the attack, the king's army set fire to all of the town's thatched-roof houses. Townspeople dragged their sick and injured into the cathedral, thinking no one could harm them there. Thirteen hundred men, women, and children huddled within the church walls.

Suddenly, a burning cinder from one of the flaming houses flew into the air and landed on the roof of the church. Within minutes, the building was completely engulfed in flames. From a hilltop outside the city, King Louis could see the massive flames leaping into the sky. He could hear the people trapped inside screaming for help. Before anything could be done to save them, however, the roof collapsed, killing everyone inside.

The guilt was too much for King Louis to bear. The cries of the people at Vitry haunted him day and night. For days, he refused to eat or drink. He prayed constantly. Impressed by King Louis's show of remorse, the pope invited him back into the Catholic Church, but this news did little to raise his spirits. Even Eleanor could not cheer him up.

PRAYERS FOR A CHILD

One man who might have been able to prevent

King Louis's outrageous behavior was his advisor, Abbot Suger. From the beginning, however, Suger sensed that Queen Eleanor and King Louis did not want his advice. He realized that King Louis was devoted to making his beautiful wife happy, and assumed he would only listen to her. Suger concentrated instead on rebuilding the Church of St. Denis. He transformed the church with architecture never before seen. Instead of stone walls, architects designed the church with high arches and intersecting vaults. The design allowed for mammoth stained-glass windows that added brilliance to a once dark, stoic church. Suger's cathedral was the first example of what came to be known as Gothic architecture.

Suger invited Queen Eleanor and King Louis to the dedication of the church on June 10, 1144. Perhaps the outing would get King Louis's mind off his grief. Queen Eleanor dressed in her most extravagant gown. Over her dress, she wore a red velvet robe, trimmed in fur. Expensive bracelets jangled on her wrists, and long pendants dangled from her ears. She carried herself like a true queen. Next to her, King Louis must have looked out of place.

Abbot Suger, advisor to King Louis, also spent a great deal of time rebuilding the Church of St. Denis. This stained glass window depicts Abbot Suger.

In his plain, gray robe, he looked more like a monk than a king.

After the ceremony, Queen Eleanor spoke to Abbot Bernard. The abbot was unimpressed by Eleanor's showy appearance and headstrong personality. He told her to concentrate more on being a dutiful wife than on affairs of church and state. Queen Eleanor did not usually like being told what to do, but she made an exception this time. She desperately wanted a child. She had been married once before. During her previous marriage, however, she had conceived once, only to miscarry. She hoped Abbot Bernard would pray for her, and perhaps her request softened the stern abbot, because he agreed.

Abbott Bernard's prayers must have helped. Within a year, at age 22, Queen Eleanor gave birth to her first daughter, Marie. She had not provided the male heir to the throne that King Louis and the kingdom wanted, but Queen Eleanor was delighted to have a child. Consumed by the demands of motherhood, Queen Eleanor stopped meddling in her husband's affairs, but it would not be long before she would once again step into her queenly role.

Test Your Knowledge

1 Queen Adelaide, Eleanor's mother-in-law,
disapproved of Eleanor's

a. religion.

b. lavish spending.

c. attitude toward her husband.

d. age.

2 King Louis spent most of his time

a. praying.

b. hunting.

c. fishing.

d. jousting.

3 Losing one's membership privileges in the
Catholic Church is known as

a. expulsion.

b. banishment.

c. excommunication.

d. deportation.

4 Suger's cathedral was the first example of
what came to be known as

a. modern architecture.

b. Medieval architecture.

c. Doric architecture.

d. Gothic architecture.

5 How old was Queen Eleanor when she gave birth to her first child?

a. 17

b. 22

c. 25

d. 30

ANSWERS: 1. b; 2. a; 3. c; 4. d; 5. b

Give Us Crosses!

The First Crusade was fought from 1096 to 1099, before Queen Eleanor was even born. Troops from Western Europe waged a war to capture the Holy Land from the Turks. The Holy Land, the ancient country of Palestine on the eastern coast of the Mediterranean Sea, includes the city of Jerusalem. Despite the fact that the

Muslims had ruled Jerusalem since 638, Christians were still allowed to continue their pilgrimages to visit the city. In the eleventh century, however, things began to change. Seljuk Turks took control of Jerusalem and forbade all Christians from entering the Holy City.

In 1095, Pope Urban II made an inspiring speech. He called upon all people in Europe—both rich and poor—to rescue the Holy Land from the Turks. Many men joined the army on a pilgrimage and war to save the Christians in the East. The First Crusade was a success. Four states, ruled by nobles from Normandy and France, were established in the Holy Land.

On December 24, 1144, Turks took over the city of Edessa, capital of one of the newly established states. The following year, a new pope, Eugenius III, sent a letter to King Louis. In the letter, he pleaded for a Second Crusade to help rescue the people of Edessa. King Louis and Queen Eleanor were celebrating Christmas at Bourges in Normandy when Pope Eugenius's letter reached them. King Louis was excited at the thought of leading the Second Crusade to Jerusalem. Without even consulting his advisors, he wrote a letter to the pope expressing his support for the mission. He would be fully committed to the cause.

On Christmas Day, King Louis announced his intentions to launch the Second Crusade. His news did not bring the enthusiasm he had hoped it would. Vassals in Aquitaine and France were reluctant to support another Crusade. About 70,000 Aquitainian countrymen and thousands of French citizens had died in the First Crusade. The long journey to the Holy Land was sure to be filled with danger.

Even faithful Suger urged King Louis to reconsider. He believed King Louis was more needed at home in France, to keep peace and govern his kingdom. In addition, King Louis had little military experience, and Suger reminded him that his previous campaigns had ended in disaster. Finally, King Louis did not have a son as an heir to the throne. If the king died in battle, the kingdom might be left vulnerable.

Much to Suger's surprise, Queen Eleanor announced that she, too, wished to join the effort. Despite the fact that no woman had ever fought

On Christmas Day 1114, King Louis VII announced his intentions to launch the Second Crusade. Saint Bernard is shown here preaching the Second Crusade, in the presence of King Louis VII.

in the Crusades, King Louis offered little resistance to his wife's request. There was a good chance Queen Eleanor could get the support of her vassals in Aquitaine, which would help King Louis tremendously. Some also believed that King Louis refused to leave Queen Eleanor at home alone because he was too jealous of her charm and beauty to go without her. Queen Eleanor and King Louis had made up their minds; they would lead the Second Crusade to the Holy Land.

During the following months, Queen Eleanor went to work recruiting her vassals. Before long, her magnetism and fervor had persuaded some of her lords to join the effort, but the army still needed many more fighters. When the royal family left Bourges, there was still some doubt about whether there would even be a Second Crusade.

Queen Eleanor refused to give up. The Second Crusade was an exciting escape from her boring castle routine. A pilgrimage to Jerusalem would bring adventure back into her life. She continued to work on the people of Aquitaine. She toured her kingdom, giving speeches, organizing supplies, and recruiting troops. Even the troubadours composed

Queen Eleanor was eager to join the Second Crusade. She believed that a pilgrimage to Jerusalem would bring adventure back into her life. A view of Jerusalem is depicted here.

songs to help build support. Before long, all of France was bustling with enthusiasm. Towns emptied as men hurried to enlist in the army.

On March 31, 1146, Easter Day, King Louis and Queen Eleanor attended a public ceremony at a hilltop church in Vezlay, France. People gathered in the surrounding field to catch a glimpse of the king and queen. The abbot gave an inspiring sermon in support of the Second Crusade. With tears running down his cheeks, King Louis stepped forward to take the cross—the emblem of the Second Crusade. The crowd shouted, "To Jerusalem!" Filled with emotion, thousands of people rushed forward. "Crosses! Give us crosses!" they exclaimed. [2]

TO JERUSALEM!

By June 1147, an army of some 100,000 men had been mounted. The largest number of soldiers came from Queen Eleanor's Aquitaine. Queen Eleanor, too, was ready to embark. Her baggage train was quite impressive. She was not about to live without her royal comforts and luxuries. Her luggage included clothes, furs, tents, jewelry, veils, beds, drinking goblets and plates, washbowls, soaps, and food. To the sounds of cheering crowds and ringing bells, two armies departed for the Holy Land.

The armies set off in separate directions. The French army, including Queen Eleanor and King Louis, headed for Regensburg in Bavaria. From there, the troops would follow the River Danube through Hungary and Bulgaria. They traveled up to 20 miles a day. One observer commented, "Anyone seeing these columns with their helmets and buckles shining in the sun, with their banners streaming in the breeze, would have been certain that they were about to triumph over all the enemies of the Cross. . . ."[3]

The second army, the Roman imperial army, was led by the German emperor, Conrad III. Emperor Conrad had marched ahead of the French army. On October 26, an eclipse of the sun blackened the sky. Many people considered this natural occurrence a sign of evil. Despite the fact that his army did not have adequate supplies, King Louis commanded his forces to continue their march south toward Jerusalem. King Louis went, instead, to Constantinople, fabled capital city of the Byzantine Empire, for supplies. There the emperor told King

King Louis VII and Emperor Conrad III enter Constantinople during the Second Crusade.

Louis that he had received word that Emperor Conrad had won a great victory over the Turks. The imperial army had reportedly killed some 14,000 Turks. King Louis was overjoyed by the news and immediately left to rejoin his troops.

At the end of October, the Crusaders met up with several hundred men from Emperor Conrad's army. The men were starving, wounded, or dying.

They told King Louis that they were all that was left of the imperial army. They told a much different story than the one King Louis had heard. Instead of gaining a victory over the Turks, they had suffered a devastating loss. More than nine-tenths of the army had been slaughtered in the attack. The survivors warned King Louis that the Turks were waiting to attack the French, as well.

King Louis was overcome with grief. Not only had many men died, but the emperor of Byzantine had seemingly betrayed him. Still, he insisted that the soldiers continue their march to the Holy Land, hoping to find more survivors along the way. On November 3, they found Emperor Conrad, seriously injured with a head wound.

All through November and December, the soldiers pressed on. They followed the south coast, through dangerous canyons and gorges. They wasted valuable time trying to find shortcuts. On one occasion, King Louis spent three days wandering away from camp in search of a shorter route, before he finally had to be guided back by a local.

On Christmas Eve, the Second Crusade celebrated its first victory in a skirmish with the Turks.

Soldiers drove the warriors into the hills and raided their deserted camp for food and gold. The victory was followed by tragedy, however. For five days, heavy rains and sleet beat down on the army. Strong winds shook the soldiers tents loose from the ground. The river flooded its banks. Some men and horses drowned, and vital food and equipment was washed away.

Suffering losses, King Louis decided the army should immediately march to Antioch, one of the Crusader states. They would take the most direct route, over the Phrygian Mountains. The soldiers had no guides to lead them. They had to use the sun and stars for direction. The journey proved rough. Turkish raiding parties constantly harassed the Crusaders, shooting at them with bows and arrows, or attacking them with saber swords. For safety, Queen Eleanor traveled in a horse-drawn litter, or cart, enclosed by leather curtains. At night, she was one of the few who took shelter in a tent. She even slept on a painted bed.

In January 1148, the Second Crusade crossed the mountains of Paphlagonia. King Louis sent ahead a small group of soldiers, along with Queen Eleanor and her vassal, Geoffrey de Rancon, to set up camp on a plateau, before the next mountain pass. When the group arrived, they found that the area was much too windswept to set up camp. Taking Queen Eleanor's advice, Geoffrey de Rancon pushed through the rocky pass and found a well-sheltered valley. Everyone thought it was a much more suitable place to camp.

When the main army arrived at the originally designated spot, they found it deserted. King Louis became alarmed when he learned that Queen Eleanor was nowhere in sight. The army continued through the pass. Suddenly, a brigade of Turks swept down on the army. Men and horses scattered in every direction. Many men plunged down a ravine to their deaths. The Turks killed some 7,000 Crusaders and plundered valuable supplies from the baggage train in the attack.

King Louis narrowly escaped death. His body-guards fell to their deaths trying to protect him. When his horse was killed beneath him, King Louis grabbed the roots of a tree and pulled himself up onto a steep rock. He gallantly held off the Turks with his back to the mountain. Darkness soon fell, and the enemy slowly retreated.

Meanwhile, Geoffrey de Rancon became nervous when the army failed to arrive at the new camp. He sent a party of knights to search for the men. They came upon the place of the slaughter and found a few survivors. As dawn broke, King Louis, blood-soaked and weary, stumbled into camp.

The king was afraid that the Turks might still be lurking in the mountains. He commanded the army to break camp at once and head for the nearest port. They would complete the journey by sea. When the army reached the port of Attalia on January 20, they were starved, dirty, and exhausted. After a five-week stay, the army finally set sail. The stormy and perilous ocean voyage lasted three weeks.

TROUBLED MARRIAGE

Raymond of Poiters, the ruler of Antioch, welcomed Queen Eleanor and King Louis. He was a tall, handsome man, gifted in conversation and familiar with the troubadours of Aquitaine. Naturally, he and Queen Eleanor immediately had a great deal in common. During the army's stay, Queen Eleanor and Raymond of Poiters spent quite a bit of time together. King Louis became jealous of the relationship and suspected they were more than just friends.

King Louis may have been right about Raymond of Poiters and Queen Eleanor. Queen Eleanor told King Louis that she wanted to stay in Antioch instead of going on to Jerusalem. If King Louis did not leave alone, she threatened to keep her vassals with her in Antioch, as well. King Louis knew that if the queen's vassals stayed behind, it would cripple the Second Crusade. King Louis fired back at his wife. He claimed he did not need her consent. As her husband, he could force her to come along.

In response, Queen Eleanor delivered some shocking news. She asked for an annulment. She wanted to end the marriage. She agreed to give up her crown and return to her duties as Duchess of Aquitaine, but for the time being, she would stay in Antioch under Raymond of Poiters's protection.

King Louis was heartbroken. He still deeply loved Queen Eleanor, but if she truly wanted a divorce, he would agree. He would, however, first need to consult with his counselors. The king's advisors forbade him from getting a divorce. They believed it would be a disgrace to him and the

French kingdom. They insisted that King Louis should force Queen Eleanor to come with him. King Louis reluctantly agreed to their plan. In the middle of the night, soldiers kidnapped Queen Eleanor, whisking her off to Jerusalem, before she could even say good-bye to Raymond of Poiters.

In May 1148, the soldiers of the Second Crusade could see the walls of Jerusalem off in the distance. Many of the soldiers dropped to their knees in prayer. On July 28, the soldiers waged their first battle against the Turks. One by one, the Crusaders died. After only four days, the French army was forced to make a humiliating retreat. This single defeat brought an end to the Second Crusade. The French were mocked by the Muslims, and their reputation around the world suffered a crushing blow.

Test Your Knowledge

1 The First Crusade was waged to
   a. capture Aquitaine from Queen Eleanor.
   b. capture the Holy Land from the Turks.
   c. capture the Vatican from the pope.
   d. capture the Holy Land from the Romans.

2 The Second Crusade was waged to
   a. help rescue the people of Edessa.
   b. establish a new capital city in the Holy Land.
   c. bring Christianity to Europe.
   d. conquer more land for France.

3 The Roman imperial army was led by
   a. Roman Emperor Augustus I.
   b. Duke Henry of Normandy.
   c. German Emperor Conrad III.
   d. Eleanor of Aquitaine.

4 During the Second Crusade about how many Crusaders were killed?
   a. 7,000
   b. 10,000
   c. 5,000
   d. 15,000

5 The soldiers of the Second Crusade reached the walls of Jerusalem in what year?

a. 1848

b. 1184

c. 1584

d. 1148

ANSWERS: 1. b; 2. a; 3. c; 4. a; 5. d

A Monk, Not a King

As fall approached, what was left of the French army began to break apart. Many soldiers deserted. King Louis bought passage back to France for those who stayed, but he and Queen Eleanor made no plans to leave anytime soon. King Louis wanted to spend Easter in the Holy Land.

During the following months, the royal couple continued to grow apart. King Louis had been deeply affected by his experiences during the Second Crusade. He spent even longer hours with his head bowed in prayer and he shaved his beard in the style of a priest. Queen Eleanor commented, "I am married to a monk, not a king."[4] King Louis felt completely hopeless about saving his marriage. Once again, he agreed to end the marriage as soon as they returned to France, but Suger cautioned the king. He reminded King Louis that he would lose valuable Aquitaine, and, furthermore, if Queen Eleanor remarried and had a son, Aquitaine would be lost forever. The argument made sense to King Louis, and he again changed his mind.

After Easter, in 1149, King Louis and Queen Eleanor left for home on separate ships. A war was being waged between Sicily and Byzantium at the time, and the queen's vessel was captured by Greek ships. The king's ship escaped and landed at Calabria, Italy. For two months, no one heard from Queen Eleanor. In a letter to Abbot Suger, King Louis explained that he had no idea whether his wife was alive or dead. Finally, King Louis received a message from King Roger of Sicily. His navy had recaptured Queen Eleanor's ship. She was ill, but recovering, in Palermo, Sicily.

King Louis and Queen Eleanor reunited and reached Italy on October 9, 1149. They traveled on to Rome, where Pope Eugenius tenderly welcomed them back. During their stay, both Queen Eleanor and King Louis confided in Pope Eugenius about their marital problems. Queen Eleanor confessed her unhappiness, but King Louis said he still loved his wife very much. The pope refused to consider an annulment. Instead he blessed the marriage and commanded them to restore their love for each other. Queen Eleanor outwardly agreed, but, in her heart, she was no longer in love with King Louis.

In August 1151, Queen Eleanor and King Louis returned to Paris. Nearly two and a half years had passed since they had seen their homeland. Their subjects welcomed the royal couple home with a grand celebration. King Louis was presented with two medals for his bravery. Deep down, however, the people were sad and angry about the disappointing outcome of the Second Crusade.

Shortly after her return, Queen Eleanor met Duke Henry of Normandy. She found herself quite attracted to him, even though he was 11 years younger than she was. King Louis, meanwhile, was growing more and more difficult to live with. The end of their marriage seemed inevitable.

Many people wondered about Queen Eleanor. She was such a beautiful woman and so open in conversation with men that some members of the royal court thought she was being unfaithful to King Louis. Most likely, Queen Eleanor never actually cheated on the king, but the fact that Queen Eleanor was unhappy in her marriage was no secret.

GETTING A DIVORCE

Queen Eleanor's chance for a divorce finally came when, on September 7, 1151, Abbot Suger died as a result of a high fever. A new abbot—Abbot St. Bernard—took his place as King Louis's advisor. Abbot St. Bernard had always been suspicious of Queen Eleanor. The contrast between the king and queen was troubling to him. King Louis, a devout follower of his religion, surrounded

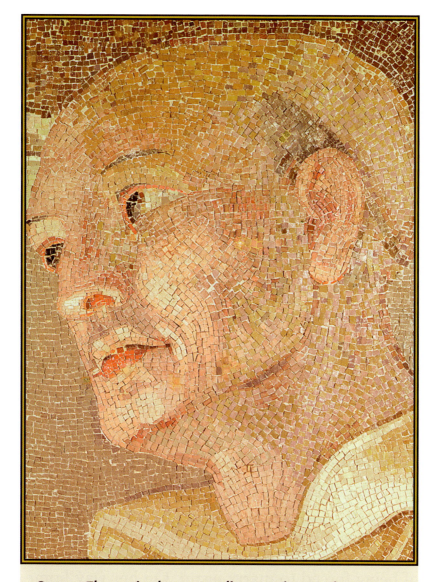

Queen Eleanor's chance to divorce King Louis came when Abbot Suger died and Abbot St. Bernard (shown here) replaced him as the king's closest advisor. Abbot St. Bernard pressured King Louis to be rid of Queen Eleanor.

himself with monks. Queen Eleanor, in contrast, was in the constant companionship of her troubadours. Such a woman was unfit to be married to such an important monarch. King Louis knew he could not just throw Queen Eleanor out, however. Her vassals in Aquitaine dearly loved her. He did not want them to revolt. If he accused Queen Eleanor of being unfaithful, she would be guilty of treason and would be sentenced to death. King Louis could not stand the thought of losing Queen Eleanor or the kingdom of Aquitaine, but Bernard pressured him to be rid of the queen. Finally, King Louis decided it was best to grant Queen Eleanor an annulment. On March 21, 1152, the marriage between King Louis and Queen Eleanor ended.

Eleanor, now Duchess of Aquitaine, immediately left for Poitiers. Once again, she was the coveted heiress of Aquitaine, but she was also in danger of being forced to marry again. On her way home, she had to escape by night on a barge down the Loire River to the town of Tours, but the danger was not over yet. At Tours, she learned that Geoffrey, a younger brother of Duke Henry, was ready to kidnap her. She again changed her route and traveled a small, wayside road. Finally, she returned safely to her palace at Poitiers.

Eleanor had broken free of her unhappy marriage, but, as her journey home showed, it appeared she was now was in an even more dangerous situation. She had once been the honored queen of France who demanded respect from her subjects. Now, it seemed, she could be kidnapped and, with a sword held to her throat, forced to marry.

Her only escape was to quickly marry a man of her own choice, so she offered her hand to Duke Henry of Normandy, who gladly accepted. Next to her former husband, King Louis, the duke was the most eligible man in France. Not only did he rule Normandy, but he had also inherited the territories of Maine, Anjou, and Touraine. He also stood a good chance of obtaining England. Duke Henry was a tall, broad, and muscular man. His short, red hair and beard showed off his fiery temprament, and his blue eyes sparkled with energy.

Only eight weeks after her annulment from King Louis, Duchess Eleanor and Duke Henry gathered at the Church of Saint Pierre in Poitiers. The 29-year-old

Duke Henry of Normandy (shown here) offered Eleanor of Aquitaine the chance to escape her unhappy marriage to King Louis. Duke Henry ruled Normandy, but he had also inherited the territories of Maine, Anjou, and Touraine.

Duchess of Aquitaine and the 18-year-old Duke of Normandy were married on March 18, 1152.

King Louis was horrified when he heard the news. He, no doubt, had expected any of Eleanor's possible suitors to ask his permission to marry her. After all, Duchess Eleanor was now under his guard and Duke Henry was his vassal. In truth, the couple was legally bound to get his approval. Nevertheless, the effects of the marriage would be catastrophic. King Louis had made a terrible political blunder. Abbot Suger's warnings had come true. Not only had King Louis let Aquitaine slip through his fingers, but, if Duke Henry took over England, he would become the most powerful ruler in Western Europe.

As usual, King Louis reacted violently and too late. He mounted an army to conquer Aquitaine. Duke Henry was off preparing to invade England when he received word that King Louis was attacking his eastern borders. The duke rushed home with ferocious speed to defend his lands. King Louis was surprised by the strength of his opponent and made a hasty retreat. After two months of fighting, King Louis agreed to a truce.

AGAIN A QUEEN

In January 1153, Duke Henry sailed for England. By July, he had taken over Wallingford and won several other campaigns. He had some support in

England because many English lords had land in Normandy. King Stephen of England was brave, but he was a poor military leader. Nonetheless, he still controlled much of England. King Stephen fought on with the hope that his oldest son, Eustace, might take over the crown. Eustace was ruthless and determined, and would make a strong adversary against Duke Henry. In the middle of August, however, Eustace choked during dinner and died. Heartbroken, King Stephen named the Duke of Normandy as his heir and future king of England.

Meanwhile, Duchess Eleanor lived in Angers, the capital of Anjou, one of the loveliest towns along the River Loire. On August 17, 1153, she gave birth to her first son. She named him William, after her father and grandfather. While Duke Henry was away, Duchess Eleanor entertained herself with famous troubadours. One of these men was Bernart de Ventadour. Like so many men who met Duchess Eleanor, Ventadour fell madly in love with her. His most admired songs were about her. Some historians believe Duchess Eleanor was also in love with him. Ventadour was so overcome with love for Duchess Eleanor that he became flustered whenever he saw her. He called her "his magnet."[5] He once told her, "You have been the first among my joys and you shall be the last, so long as there is life in me."[6] His songs were so fluid and beautiful, they must have mesmerized Duchess Eleanor and her court. When Duke Henry learned of the troubadour's affection for his wife, he summoned Ventadour to England at once to keep him away from Duchess Eleanor. Ventadour was so in love with Eleanor, he could find no one to replace her memory. He died having become a monk.

Duke Henry returned from England in 1154. On October 25, King Stephen died. The English throne was passed on to Duke Henry, who would become King Henry. Harsh weather kept Henry from claiming his new kingdom, however. The terrible weather lasted for a month. Meanwhile, Henry grew horribly impatient and could wait no longer. Finally, despite nasty winds, he set sail with Eleanor. The perilous voyage surely reminded Eleanor of the Crusades. Strong winds and dense fog caused their ship to separate

(continued on page 64)

The Courts of Love

Eleanor of Aquitaine is probably most famous for her "courts of love." Men would come to these courts with their love problems. Eleanor and other high-class ladies would hear their troubles and offer advice. Most people believe the courts of love are just a legend and that Eleanor of Aquitaine did not preside over an actual court. She probably did not hear real cases nor make legal judgments, but the troubadours of Eleanor's court were real, and many of their songs took the form of a game, which ended with the advice of a great lady.

The game consisted of a two-part song. In the first stanza, one troubadour would sing about a problem he had with his lady love. Another troubadour would offer his opinion in the second stanza. The two performers repeated the song over and over again. Usually, neither singer could decide what to do, so the troubadours would ask Eleanor and her court what to do.

Troubadours expressed an undying devotion to a lady of Eleanor of Aquitaine's stature—much beyond their reach. They performed a "service of love." The relationship to their lady was much like that of a vassal to his overlord. Eleanor of Aquitaine was the lady of many troubadours, but other great ladies also visited her court, including duchesses, countesses, and even Louis VII's daughter Alice.

At court, troubadours wore expensive clothes in colors that matched their moods. Young men grew their hair long and dressed in long cloaks with flowing sleeves. The women wore gowns with long trains that dragged behind them when they walked.

Eleanor of Aquitaine is said to have taught crude men how to be gentlemen. She ushered in the age of chivalry—when brave knights protected women from danger. In Eleanor's court, women were superior to men, a fact that should not come as a surprise. After all, at the time, Queen Eleanor was struggling to gain her independence from King Henry. No matter what went on in her life, Queen Eleanor certainly loved her court of troubadours. It was the one place she could escape the harsh reality of her life and exert the power and authority she so desperately desired.

(continued from page 61)

from the rest of the fleet. After 24 hours of tossing on stormy seas, Queen Eleanor and King Henry made it safely to shore near Southampton. At last, they were crowned the king and queen of England.

Test Your Knowledge

1 After Easter, in 1149, Queen Eleanor's ship
was captured by
   a. English ships.
   b. Greek ships.
   c. Spanish ships.
   d. Italian ships.

2 Duke Henry of Normandy was how many
years younger than Queen Eleanor?
   a. 11
   b 15
   c. 8
   d. 10

3 In what year did Eleanor give birth to her
first son?
   a. 1355
   b. 1531
   c. 1153
   d. 1145

4 Bernart de Ventadour called Eleanor
   a. "his inspiration."
   b. "his sunshine."
   c. "his anchor."
   d. "his magnet."

5 Duke Henry became king in what year?

    a. 1154

    b. 1454

    c. 1145

    d. 1545

ANSWERS: 1. b; 2. a; 3. c; 4. d; 5. a

Queen Eleanor and Her Sons

King Stephen's reign had left much of England in terrible disorder. King Henry went to work cleaning it up right away. Queen Eleanor admired her husband's energy and fresh ideas. They were an exciting change from Louis's serious manner, but Henry could be a highly unpredictable king. He was always leaving in the early morning hours or changing his mind at the last minute. His whims could throw the royal court into complete chaos. One official described him as a "lively imitation of hell."[7]

The king was also a relentless traveler, and Queen Eleanor accompanied him on many trips. Queen Eleanor journeyed countless miles on horseback, over crude roads and rough terrain. Some days, King Henry covered more than five times the distance of the average man, traveling probably as far as 40 miles. On these trips, Queen Eleanor met many of the great Englishmen of her day. She visited earls, counts, and dukes. King Henry and Queen Eleanor were close to all of the important church officials—including archbishops and bishops. The friendships were not formed because the king was overly religious, but because the leaders of the church were also his advisors and administrators. One of these men was Deacon Thomas Becket. King Henry was immediately impressed with Becket and named him chancellor, the king's closest advisor. Becket would become King Henry's greatest source of delight and his deepest source of pain.

For the next 13 years, Queen Eleanor was often pregnant. She and King Henry had five sons— William (who died at age three), Henry, Richard, Geoffrey, and John. They also had three daughters—

A Descendent of the Devil

Because Queen Eleanor had so much trouble conceiving children—especially a son—with Louis VII, she believed their marriage was cursed by God, but King Henry's family was believed to have been cursed, as well. One of King Henry's ancestors, Count Fulk Nerra the Black, was a cruel warlord, who brutally murdered and tortured his enemies. According to legend, the count married an evil spirit named Melusine—the daughter of Satan. After having her children, she flew back to hell. For this reason, some people thought King Henry was a descendent of the devil.

This legend obviously did not scare Queen Eleanor. She and King Henry had eight children together. Her pregnancies probably confirmed her belief that her first marriage was cursed. In fact, three of her boys became kings and two girls became queens, but her children's lives were far from trouble-free.

Matilda, Eleanor, and Joanna. Eleanor's first daughter with Louis, Princess Margaret, was being raised in England, but King Louis refused to let Eleanor see her. Little is known about Eleanor's early relationships with her children.

According to the customs of the time, the children would have grown up away from their mother. Usually, the children lived in the homes of trusted, well-known business people. However, Queen Eleanor probably saw Richard often. From the cradle, Richard was named as heir to Aquitaine. He was Eleanor's hope of regaining power. From age 12 on, Richard was Eleanor's constant companion. Nevertheless, all of her children loved her dearly.

BURNING FOR POWER

As queen of England, Eleanor regained the respect and glory she had lost as a result of her divorce. On the other hand, she now had much less power than she had when she was King Louis's wife. Eleanor was entitled to special payments of queen's gold and she issued her special seal to any official documents when King Henry was out of the kingdom. The real rulers in King Henry's absence, however, were the justiciars, the judges of the English courts. Queen Eleanor soon realized that she would be unable to control King Henry's decisions. As a commanding and intelligent woman, however, she surely grew tired of being tamed.

An even greater disappointment to Queen Eleanor was the fact that King Henry ruled Aquitaine alone. King Louis VII had never dared to rule Eleanor's beloved Aquitaine. The current situation no doubt frustrated the independent queen, who felt it was her right to rule her own land. In many ways, her strong-willed nature clashed with King Henry's domineering personality, but she decided to wait—in the hope that her son Richard would one day help her recover some of her political power. In the meantime, she tried to enjoy her life of extravagance.

Strangely enough, Thomas Becket turned out to be Queen Eleanor's first rival for Henry's attention. Becket was quick-witted and intelligent, which made him amusing to talk to. King Henry and Thomas Becket spent entire days together—hunting, playing chess, and discussing business. King Henry trusted Becket so much that he put him in charge of raising the heir to the thrown—young Henry. Despite the fact that Henry was 16 years younger than Becket, the two men developed a strong friendship. In later years, however, their relationship turned disagreeable. Thomas Becket became an archbishop and worked as a champion of the Catholic Church. The two men often disagreed, and Becket defied King Henry's rule on more than one occasion.

The brotherly affection between her husband and Thomas Becket must have fueled Queen Eleanor's jealously. Above all, she certainly resented Becket for taking over the power she had wanted for herself—being the second most important person in the kingdom. Queen Eleanor was too smart, however, to openly show her dislike for Becket. Such an action would put the king's affection for her—and her access to more power—at risk.

Meanwhile, Eleanor's former husband, King Louis, remarried. King Louis took Spain's Princess Constance of Castile as his second bride. Much to King Louis's disappointment, during their marriage she gave birth to two more daughters. King Louis still did not have a son who would become an heir to the throne.

henriaus natus. matilde regna tenebat
sub quo sagratus thomas martyre radebat.

henricus rex filius   matildis imperatus geni

henr
haueni
regis qui
obiit

King Henry and Thomas Becket developed a close friendship. In later years, however, their relationship turned
disagreeable. King Henry (left) is shown here arguing with
Thomas Becket (right).

Both King Louis and King Henry understood how
important it was to create peace between their kingdoms. They shared borders, and neither one wanted
the other causing trouble. In September 1158, King
Henry traveled to Paris to discuss the situation with
King Louis. During his visit, King Henry arranged a
marriage between his son Henry and King Louis's

daughter Marguerite, from his second marriage. Strangely, King Henry and King Louis struck up a friendship. The arranged marriage was a triumph for Eleanor. She had always hoped to have a son who would become the king of France. On November 2, 1160, five-year-old Henry and five-year-old Marguerite were married. Marriages between very young children were quite common among royal arranged marriages, which were more about politics and securing kingdoms than about true love.

Soon, however, King Henry and Queen Eleanor had reason to worry. When King Louis's second wife, Constance, died, he hastily married Adela Champagne. On August 22, 1165, Adela Champagne gave birth to a long-awaited son and future king, Philip II. The baby was a bitter disappointment for Queen Eleanor. His birth meant that none of her sons would ever be king of France.

FAIR ROSAMUND

King Henry was known for his many mistresses, but his most famous love affair was with Rosamund Clifford. Young and beautiful, she was known to many as "Fair Rosamund." King Henry did not try to hide his affection for Rosamund. In fact, he paraded her around England openly and publicly. He let Rosamund live in Queen Eleanor's royal apartments. Much to Queen Eleanor's disgust, Rosamund became a direct rival for the king's attention.

On one hand, the affair no doubt turned Queen Eleanor against King Henry. On the other hand, however, it also allowed the queen to make plans of her own. About this time, Queen Eleanor began plotting to overthrow her husband. Her secret scheme would take years of careful preparation. Wanting to spend time with Rosamund, King Henry thought it was best for Queen Eleanor to leave England. He allowed her to go home to Aquitaine. Eleanor was happy to return to her beautiful homeland. In early 1168, Eleanor returned to Poitou, where she would spend the next five years of her life.

From time to time, King Henry visited Aquitaine to check up on Queen Eleanor. While he was there, he governed the kingdom personally. Queen Eleanor must have been furious with King Henry's decision to rule the kingdom personally. It severely lessened her power in her own land. Either the king did not seem to notice Queen Eleanor's anger, or he chose to ignore it. Queen Eleanor probably hid her true feelings from her husband. Instead, she traveled throughout Aquitaine and Poitou, visiting lords and manners. At each stop, she formed alliances with her vassals. In return, they vowed their loyalty to Queen Eleanor, not to her husband, the king of England.

MEETING AT MONTMIRAIL

In January 1169, King Henry II of England and King Louis VII of France met at Montmirail in Maine to negotiate a lasting peace agreement between the two nations. For two years, they had been at war with each other. The main point of business was to get King Louis's approval on equitable distribution of land. King Henry made arrangements to divide his empire among his sons. Much to King Henry's delight, King Louis agreed. Queen Eleanor, of course, was not consulted on the matter, but with these plans, she must have seen her opportunity to overthrow her husband and regain complete independence.

Queen Eleanor and King Henry's oldest son and heir, Henry, was going to inherit England, Normandy, Maine, and Anjou. This was the land

Thomas Becket departs from King Henry II of England and King Louis VII of France. Following the breakdown of negotiations at Montmirail, Becket joined the common people.

that King Henry II had received from his father. Young Henry would also become an overlord to Brittany. On May 24, 1170, the 15-year-old was crowned as future king. At the coronation banquet, the outgoing king waited on the new king. The archbishop of York commented that no prince in the world was ever waited on by the king. To this, the boy replied, "Is it not fitting that the son of a mere count should wait on the son of a king?"[8] His reaction showed his conceit and ungrateful nature, but Eleanor was pleased by her son's coronation.

His new crown might help her tip the balance of power against her husband. Eleanor was already working to turn her son against his father.

Geoffrey became heir to Brittany. He would be a vassal to young King Henry. Geoffrey also grew up to become one of the most evil of King Henry's sons. He once boasted that it was the family tradition for brother to hate brother and for a son to turn against his father. The fact that he had no problem rebelling against his father worked in Queen Eleanor's favor.

Richard, Queen Eleanor's favorite son, was, of course, heir to Aquitaine. That left Eleanor and Henry's fourth son, John, with nothing. The king jokingly named him "Lackland," but Henry intended to give the boy an inheritance at a later time.

None of Queen Eleanor's daughters played a part in the queen's grand scheme. Matilda married Henry of Saxony, a German prince, in 1168. Young Eleanor married Alfonso VIII of Castile in 1170. Joanna, the youngest, married William II of Sicily in 1177.

Meanwhile, King Henry II had taken over Ireland. His kingdom now stretched across two seas, making it difficult to govern such a large area. Throughout Europe, his vassals became increasingly unruly. Hardly a day went by without a revolt in some corner of his empire. Queen Eleanor probably thought her husband had spread his power too thin. She saw her chance to set her plan in motion. Too many revolts at once would bring King Henry's realm crashing down around him. A successful revolt, however, would require allies who had a common ground, who could come together in a carefully planned campaign. By 1173, Queen Eleanor found those allies in her sons.

Young Henry, then 18, was tall and handsome, brave and energetic. He was charming and generous, but also unstable and unreliable. His wild behavior at jousting competitions and parties attracted a following of rowdy young men. The elder King Henry showed the young king outward respect, but refused to give him any real power. When young Henry's father was away, justiciars still ruled the kingdom. Young Henry came to bitterly resent his father's lack of confidence in him.

Richard, Count of Poitou, was 16. He was stocky and strong, bold and daring, and an excellent horseman and soldier. Although he had much respect and affection for his mother, Queen Eleanor, he could sometimes be violent and cruel. He had little love for his father and he wanted more power and independence.

Eleanor's third son, Geoffrey, was only 15. Many people described him as thoroughly evil. He had dark hair and he was shorter than both Henry and Richard. He was perhaps the most intelligent sibling of the family, but also the least worthy of trust. John, Eleanor's youngest son, had not yet inherited any land. He would be of no use in Eleanor's power play.

Queen Eleanor's plan was ready. She decided that, as young as they were, her three oldest sons were capable of leading a revolt against their father, the king.

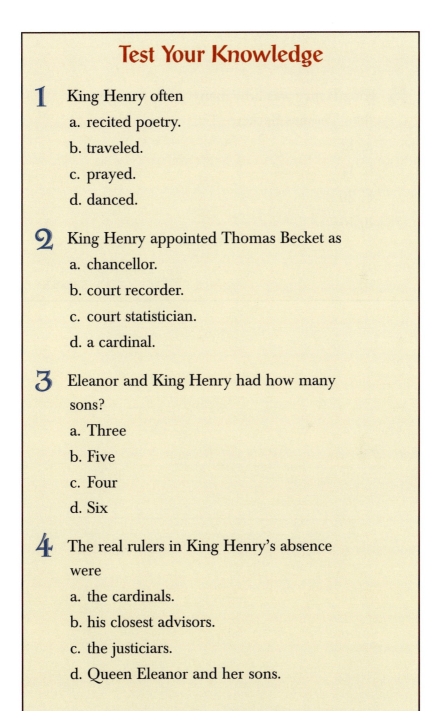

Test Your Knowledge

1 King Henry often
   a. recited poetry.
   b. traveled.
   c. prayed.
   d. danced.

2 King Henry appointed Thomas Becket as
   a. chancellor.
   b. court recorder.
   c. court statistician.
   d. a cardinal.

3 Eleanor and King Henry had how many sons?
   a. Three
   b. Five
   c. Four
   d. Six

4 The real rulers in King Henry's absence were
   a. the cardinals.
   b. his closest advisors.
   c. the justiciars.
   d. Queen Eleanor and her sons.

5 King Henry was how many years younger
than Thomas Becket?

　　a. 12

　　b. 14

　　c. 20

　　d. 16

ANSWERS: 1. b; 2. a; 3. b; 4. c; 5. d

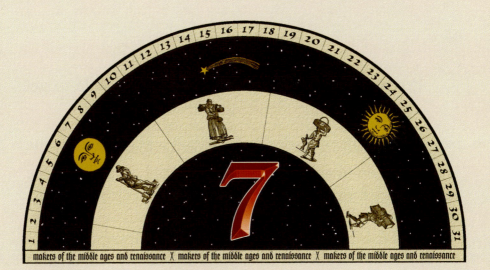

Queen Eleanor's Revolt

The revolt of 1173 against King Henry II was a well-planned scheme, and Queen Eleanor was the driving force behind the ingenious plot. Her basic plan granted her sons power in their rightful lands. With his lands divided among his sons, King Henry would be too weak to force the princes to follow his orders.

Perhaps Queen Eleanor would even be able to get rid of King Henry for good.

The queen's prize in the revolt was Aquitaine. She intended to rule through, and with, her favorite son, Richard. Her plan probably would have unfolded without a hitch, if young Henry had not faltered.

Until the revolt broke out, King Henry had no idea that his wife was plotting against him. A woman planning a conspiracy was unheard of. Women of that time did not play a leading role in politics, but Queen Eleanor was the exception. Her plan failed, but not because of any shortcomings on her part. She simply had terrible luck against a skillful opponent.

Meanwhile, Eleanor's former husband, King Louis VII, also became a valuable ally. Over the years, he had matured into a respected statesman. King Louis was annoyed with King Henry's vast empire. He encouraged young Henry to demand at least one of the kingdoms he had been promised. Young Henry took King Louis's advice. He demanded control over England, Normandy, or Anjou. The outburst caused King Henry to suspect foul play. He accused King Louis of trying to make trouble between father and son. At first, King Henry thought he would imprison young Henry to keep him out of trouble, but, instead, he simply had guards keep an eye on him.

On the night of March 7, 1173, young Henry got his guards drunk and escaped. He fled to Paris to find safety with King Louis. Young Henry's actions proved to his father that his suspicions about foul play were real—no doubt, dooming Queen Eleanor's scheme to failure. King Henry sent ambassadors to Paris to bring his son home. When the ambassadors arrived and announced that the king had sent them, King Louis replied:

> Impossible. The king of England is with me. You are quite wrong in giving the title to his father. That king is dead, and it would be as well if he ceased to think of himself as a king, since before all the world he has handed over his kingdom to his son.[9]

Young Henry called a group of English noblemen to Paris. They swore to fight for the new king. In turn, young Henry promised to get their approval before making any peace agreements. He formed alliances with the Count of Flanders and the Count of Blois. They all declared young Henry III as the rightful king of England. Queen Eleanor encouraged Richard and Geoffrey to join their brother in Paris. The young new king also found allies throughout his father's empire. He had support in almost every domain. Queen Eleanor and her sons hoped to strip the elder King Henry of power in every kingdom he ruled, except Normandy.

The plan probably would have worked perfectly, if young Henry had not inadvertently alerted his father to their intentions. Because he was alerted to foul play, the elder king, Henry II, had time to prepare. Most of the fighting took place in Normandy, where a large number of knights remained loyal to the elder king. Henry II pushed the French invading army out of Normandy. Throughout the realm, the king's supporters scattered rebel fighters. By the summer of 1174, young Henry's support system was completely broken.

On September 8, a peace conference took place. King Henry II was generous with his rebellious sons. Young Henry remained the heir to the throne, and Geoffrey and Richard were forgiven because of their young age. However, King Henry insisted that his youngest son, John, now his favorite, and the only son not to be involved in the plot against his father, would receive lands on both sides of the English Channel—in England and in France.

Meanwhile, Queen Eleanor had been held captive for over a year. In August 1173, her husband fought in Poitou, and Queen Eleanor fled to her uncle's castle. When the castle fell to King Henry's soldiers, Eleanor escaped just in time and set out for Paris. By chance, on the road to Chartres, some of King Henry's troops stopped a group of knights who were on their way to Paris. Queen Eleanor was with them, disguised as a nobleman, riding astride on her horse. For the next few months, Queen Eleanor was held captive in a tower in her husband's Castle of Chinon in Touraine.

(continued on page 90)

Dynamic Damsels

Eleanor of Aquitaine was unlike most women of the Middle Ages. Her intelligence, wit, and sophistication were unmatched by other women of her time. She cared little about what society expected of her and she carried herself with confidence and authority. During the Renaissance, many women decided to stand up and get noticed— much like Eleanor of Aquitaine. They, however, lived at a time when new ideas were bursting from every social circle. Some women took this opportunity to break free from their traditional roles to become dynamic damsels of history—much like Eleanor of Aquitaine had done during the Middle Ages.

Queen Isabella of Spain insisted that she and her husband, King Ferdinand, would rule their country equally. She played an important role in the course of history. Her jewels paid for Christopher Columbus's epic journey to America. Queen Isabella opened the door to other female intellectuals, and welcomed them into her royal court, but she did have a cruel side. Queen Isabella was absolutely intolerant of other races and religions. She wanted to rid Spain of anyone she believed was of a lower class. She supported the Spanish Inquisition, successfully banishing Jews, Moors, and Gypsies from the country.

Charlotte Guillard inherited Soliel d'Or—a publishing house—when her husband died suddenly. She worked tirelessly to expand her business and make it the most prestigious publishing house in Paris. She hired women as editors and published long lists of reference books, textbooks, and humanist histories. Today, the company she started is still in business.

Some people consider Queen Elizabeth I to be the greatest of all British rulers. By the time she was eight years old, she had already lived through incredible turmoil. The church accused her mother of having an affair and claimed that Elizabeth was not the king's daughter. In anger, King Henry VIII had Elizabeth's mother beheaded. When Elizabeth's half sister, Mary Tudor, took the throne, she had Elizabeth imprisoned in the Tower of London. Elizabeth finally became queen when she was 25 years old. During her 45-year reign, England thrived culturally, economically, and politically. She introduced many reforms, including a social welfare plan. She died in 1603, never having married nor given birth to an heir.

One of the most exciting women of the time was Grace O'Malley, a pirate. Grace O'Malley sailed the high seas along the Irish coast, harassing English ships and stealing from other pirates. One of her sons and a brother were captured by the English and imprisoned. Grace O'Malley paid a personal visit to Queen Elizabeth to bargain for their release. The queen was so impressed by Grace O'Malley's confidence and courage, she granted both men pardons.

(continued from page 87)

PRISONER OF THE KING

King Henry's anger with Queen Eleanor must have been incredible. Her years of secret planning were now out in the open. King Henry could not believe that his wife would turn their sons against him. In July 1174, he sent Eleanor as a prisoner to Old Sarum Castle. Today, on the site where the tower once stood, a ring around a grassy mound is still visible. This mark is all that is left of the castle.

King Henry II was unsure of what to do with his treacherous wife. At first, he wanted to divorce her. Letting Queen Eleanor go free, however, posed serious problems. The king would be making the same mistake that King Louis had made nearly 25 years earlier. King Henry agreed to divorce Queen Eleanor if she would abandon the world and vow to become a nun, but Eleanor was a shrewd woman who refused to give up her rights. She remained a captive.

At age 53, Queen Eleanor was considered old in the twelfth century. With her plans in ruins, it seemed as though she had no hope left, but the determined queen refused to give up. She continued to believe there might still be a chance that she could regain even just a sliver of power. First, however, she would have to endure 15 years of imprisonment.

Queen Eleanor was moved to several different castles during her imprisonment, but her situation remained much the same. The castles were all too heavily guarded for her to escape. During her captivity, Queen Eleanor knew little about what was going on in the outside world.

Meanwhile, with Queen Eleanor tucked away and guarded, King Henry was free to carry on an even more open affair with Rosamund. His mistress did not enjoy her royal role for long, however. In 1176, she became ill and died soon after. King Henry was crushed. Fair Rosamund had been the love of his life. Although he continued to have other mistresses, none would ever take her place in his heart.

In 1179, Richard was installed as Duke of Aquitaine. King Henry allowed Queen Eleanor to attend the ceremony. She spoke out publicly against King Henry's rule and declared Richard the rightful ruler of Aquitaine. After the ceremony, Queen Eleanor again became a prisoner of the king.

At the end of 1179, Queen Eleanor's first husband, Louis VII, became paralyzed as a result of a severe stroke. He lingered in that condition for a year, but died in September 1180. Locked in a castle tower, Queen Eleanor probably knew nothing about his death.

SQUABBLING SONS

After joining forces against their father, Eleanor's sons had little family loyalty. They began fighting among themselves. In 1182, young King Henry III, together with his brother Geoffrey, invaded Poitou against Richard. The attack sparked a full-scale civil war.

Young King Henry's army—probably consisting of many of young Henry's troublemaking friends—brought chaos to the people of Poitou. They plundered villages and ransacked churches. The elder King Henry tried to maintain peace between his sons, but they ignored him. Young Henry eventually became ill, and his resources began to run out. His few faithful followers did not even have enough money to buy food.

In June 1183, Queen Eleanor had a vivid dream. She saw her son, young King Henry, lying on a bed. His hands were folded on his chest, as if he were laid out in death. On his finger was a big, bright sapphire ring. He had two crowns on his head. One was his royal crown, the other was a circle of glowing light. A few days later, Queen Eleanor got the news that young Henry had died on June 11. Apparently, when young Henry realized that he was dying, he sent a messenger to his father. He wanted to beg for his father's forgiveness. In reply, Henry II sent his son a sapphire ring, as a token of love.

Queen Eleanor took the news with bravery and self-control, but, for years, she felt the pain of loss. King Henry plunged into misery. Despite the young king's rebellion and betrayals, the elder king deeply loved his eldest son.

On his deathbed, young Henry made a dying request. He asked his father to release Queen Eleanor from captivity. The elder king could not consent, but he must have been somewhat moved by young Henry's last wish, for he allowed his daughter Matilda to see Queen Eleanor at Old Sarum. In June 1184, King Henry permitted Queen Eleanor to visit Matilda's newborn son.

On November 30, 1184, King Henry invited Queen Eleanor to spend Christmas with him. John and Richard, now heirs to the throne, also joined them. King Henry's invitation was probably not an act of forgiveness. Instead, he most likely wanted Queen Eleanor to support him in a new inheritance arrangement. After young Henry's death, the elder king's land had to be redistributed among his three living sons. King Henry II wanted to give a larger share to John, his favorite son. Given her affection for Richard, however, Queen Eleanor was little help.

King Henry wanted Richard to move to Normandy and give Aquitaine to John. Richard stubbornly refused. He had grown to love Aquitaine. On Henry's command, John and Geoffrey invaded Poitou. Richard, an excellent soldier, easily stomped out the invasion. Later, Richard went to England to pledge his loyalty to King Henry, but still refused to give up Aquitaine. Finally, King Henry forced him to hand over the rule to his mother. As it turned out, King Henry had made a smart decision. Both Richard and his vassals were still devoted to Queen Eleanor, but Richard, hungry for power, continued to rule the kingdom. In 1186, Queen Eleanor suffered another loss when her third son, Geoffrey, died. Now only two sons remained—her beloved Richard and Henry's favored John.

On November 30, 1184, King Henry invited Queen Eleanor to spend Christmas with him. John and Richard, now heirs to the throne, also joined them. John is shown here hunting.

A SHAMEFUL END

The final years of King Henry's reign were sad and troubled. He watched his sons engage in constant quarrels. Somehow, he always believed his sons would change. Yet, time and time again, their bitterness toward him—and each other—surprised him.

The new French king, Philip II, grew into a great politician. He was both brilliant and ruthless. He managed to turn Richard against his father once again. Richard insisted that King Henry guarantee that Richard was heir to the throne. He asked for full possession of Anjou, Maine, and Touraine, as well as Poitou. The king refused all of his demands. In defiance, Richard proclaimed himself as king, as well as King Philip's vassal. To King Henry's disgust and disappointment, Richard had pledged all loyalty to the king of France.

Fighting broke out in June 1189. During the war, King Henry became seriously ill with blood poisoning. Barely able to stay on his horse, he agreed to end the war. He granted his enemies all of their demands. King Henry bent down to give Richard the kiss of peace. He whispered in his ear, "God grant that I don't die before I can take my revenge on you." [10] Unfortunately, the dying king's wish would not come to fruition.

On his deathbed, King Henry learned that even his favorite son, John, had crossed over to the enemy. Deeply shamed, he turned his face to the wall and uttered his last words, "Shame, shame on a conquered king." [11] When King Henry died, on July 6, 1189, finally, Queen Eleanor's master plan was fulfilled.

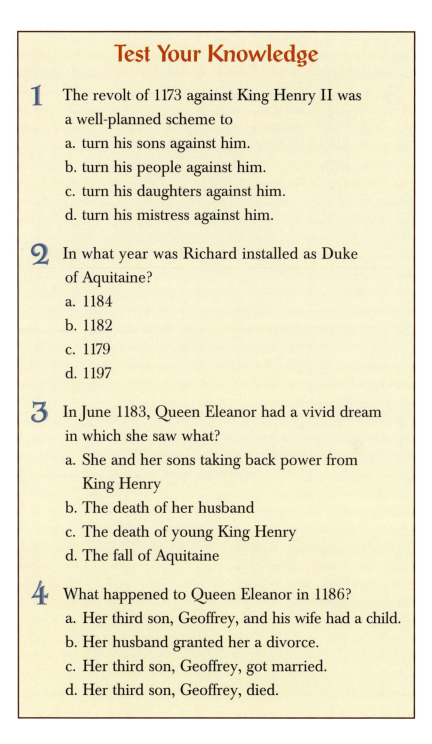

Test Your Knowledge

1 The revolt of 1173 against King Henry II was a well-planned scheme to

a. turn his sons against him.

b. turn his people against him.

c. turn his daughters against him.

d. turn his mistress against him.

2 In what year was Richard installed as Duke of Aquitaine?

a. 1184

b. 1182

c. 1179

d. 1197

3 In June 1183, Queen Eleanor had a vivid dream in which she saw what?

a. She and her sons taking back power from King Henry

b. The death of her husband

c. The death of young King Henry

d. The fall of Aquitaine

4 What happened to Queen Eleanor in 1186?

a. Her third son, Geoffrey, and his wife had a child.

b. Her husband granted her a divorce.

c. Her third son, Geoffrey, got married.

d. Her third son, Geoffrey, died.

5 In what year did King Henry die?

   a. 1243

   b. 1189

   c. 1879

   d. 1148

ANSWERS: 1. a; 2. c; 3. c; 4. d; 5. b

The Mother Queen

After hearing of his father's death, Richard suddenly felt sorry for turning against him. He bitterly mourned King Henry's death. As king, however, Richard's first task was to order his mother's release from captivity. When the king's messenger arrived at the castle where Eleanor was being held captive, he found that she had already freed herself. She was no longer being guarded or under any restrictions. He described her as "more a great lady than ever." [12] King Richard directed his messenger to give his mother anything she wanted and obey her every word. The 67-year-old queen immediately gathered her court together and traveled from city to city, castle to castle, just as she pleased.

In an outrageously lavish coronation ceremony, Richard was crowned as king of England on September 3, 1189. The crown was so heavy that two earls had to hold it over the new king's head. King Richard was a much different ruler than his father had been. In many ways, he resembled an Aquitainian robber more than a nobleman. He was cruel and he enjoyed the thrill of battle and plunder. He was happiest when he was at war. At the same time, he was a poet and a troubadour, like his great-grandfather, William IX. He also liked to show off his wealth with fancy clothes. King Richard had little love for England, which he had hardly visited since birth. Still, the English people cheered their new king. Any change from King Henry's harsh rule was a change for the better.

Richard was crowned as king of England on September 3, 1189. King Richard is shown here with his barons.

Richard was totally devoted to his masterful mother. Queen Eleanor, in turn, knew just how to control him. Even at age 67, Queen Eleanor looked strangely young. In those days, it was unusual for a woman to keep such a youthful appearance. Perhaps the forced rest that Eleanor had received as a prisoner had helped to preserve her youth. Once again, Queen Eleanor enjoyed extravagant dresses made with expensive silks, and trimmed with sable and squirrel fur.

Queen Eleanor's clothing was not the only thing that was restored to her. Much to her delight, King Richard gave her full authority over his ministers and advisors, something his father had never done. The new king also took good care of his surviving brother. He wanted to make sure that John remained his ally, not his enemy. Richard showered his brother with presents. He gave him castles and estates all over England. He also selected a bride for John— Isabella of Gloucester. She was the greatest heiress in the land. King Richard did have one condition. John was not allowed to step foot in England for three years.

KING RICHARD'S CRUSADE

King Richard became obsessed with the Crusades in the Holy Land. To raise money for an expedition, he put estates and land up for sale throughout England. By spring 1190, he had raised enough money for a fleet of about 8,000 men to set sail. Richard attended a council in France. Meanwhile,

King Richard became obsessed with the Crusades in the Holy Land. He achieved great success there. A kneeling Crusader is shown here with his horse behind him.

Eleanor convinced King Richard to take back his order and let John come to England. King Richard and King Philip discussed their plans. On June 24, 1190, the new king said good-bye to his mother. The soldiers shared tearful farewells with their families as they set off for the Holy Land.

While King Richard was away, Queen Eleanor kept busy. She traveled to Pamplona, Spain, where she called on King Sancho the Wise of Navarre. On King Richard's behalf, she asked for the hand of his daughter Berengaria in marriage. Richard had met Berengaria previously and was impressed by her intelligence. Princess Berengaria was fond of troubadours, and, therefore, was the perfect woman in Queen Eleanor's eyes.

Years earlier, Alice of France had been promised to Richard, but Eleanor wanted to stop that marriage from taking place. She wanted King Richard and Princess Berengaria to marry as soon as possible. She, no doubt, hoped the couple would have a son as an heir to the throne. No one knows for sure what Richard's private feelings were about the marriage, but he was not about to go against his mother's wishes.

Queen Eleanor and Princess Berengaria set off at once to meet King Richard. They rode over the Alps and charmed the people on the Italian peninsula. King Richard, who had sailed for the Holy Land on March 30, 1191, missed their arrival in Sicily, but he sent a ship to get the two women. Because it was Lent, Christian custom forbade the couple from getting married, but Richard promised his mother he would marry Princess Berengaria as soon as he could.

Queen Eleanor set off again for the long journey home. She arrived in Rome on Easter Sunday. From there, she crossed the Alps and continued to Rouen. The trip followed almost exactly the same route she had taken with her former husband, King Louis, some 42 years earlier.

In the meantime, King Richard's fleet was scattered by a storm off the coast of Cyprus. Some vessels crashed into the rocky shore and became shipwrecked. The people of Cyprus imprisoned any survivors. They also captured Princess Berengaria's ship. Outraged, King Richard landed his troops and, within days, took over the entire island. He married Princess Berengaria on May 12. After a three-day celebration, the Crusade left Cyprus for Acre. The troops swiftly attacked the great Palestinian seaport.

WHILE THE KING WAS AWAY

With King Richard away, his throne was in danger. Queen Eleanor found herself defending the English crown against both her youngest son, John, and King Philip of France. As it turned out, Queen Eleanor made a big mistake when she talked Richard into letting John back into England. John was determined to get his hands on part of England, if not all of it. He convinced himself that King Richard was never coming back from the Holy Land. He hoped to make the people of England believe this, as well.

John rode throughout the kingdom, making himself known to the people. He tried to make friends with people from all classes—rich and poor, nobleman and commoner. He started rumors indicating that King Richard would never return from the Crusades, and that John was now their new king.

To make matters worse, King Philip of France returned early from the Crusade, around Christmas

1191. During the battle of Acre, he fell terribly ill and lost all of his hair. King Philip used his illness to release him from his obligation to the Crusade. He had other plans. He hoped to take advantage of King Richard's absence.

Back in France, King Philip immediately increased the size of his army. By January 20, 1192, the king of France led an attack on Gisors, part of the precious Vixen territory, along the border of Normandy. For years, King Philip had wanted to regain control of this area. He invited John to France and asked him to join the revolt. In return for his support, King Philip offered French lands to John. John immediately assembled an army.

Queen Eleanor quickly took action. She alerted frontier garrisons, or forts, in Normandy, Brittany, Anjou, Poitou, and Aquitaine to a possible attack. She also warned King Philip that trying to take land from a Crusader would break the "truce of God." Bowing to Eleanor's argument, King Philip reluctantly retreated. On February 11, Queen Eleanor took a ship across the English Channel before John had a chance to come to her. She did not waste any time arguing with John. Instead, she called a great council. She gained unanimous support from the high officials in every kingdom. Facing such opposition, John had no choice but to tame his greed. For the time being, John and King Philip were taken care of.

Meanwhile, King Richard had achieved great success in the Holy Land. In just a few weeks, his troops had captured Acre. He had ambitions to take over the entire Latin kingdom. He stayed for a year, trying to accomplish his grand plan.

In September 1191, the Crusaders won a great victory near Arsuf, Israel. Soldiers marched on to Jerusalem, which they planned to take in November, but winter rains ruined King Richard's campaign. King Richard was forced to negotiate peace with the sultan. The two rulers could not come to an agreement, however. In August, the Crusade conquered Jaffa, but King Richard became ill shortly afterward. Unable to maintain his stronghold, King Richard finally agreed to a three-year peace agreement. The agreement granted Christians limited access to the Holy City of Jerusalem. Finally, on October 9, 1192, King Richard left Palestine.

King Richard wanted to return home as quickly as possible. He had received letters from his mother about King Philip's invasion and John's plot for the throne. Suddenly, the unthinkable happened. King Richard disappeared.

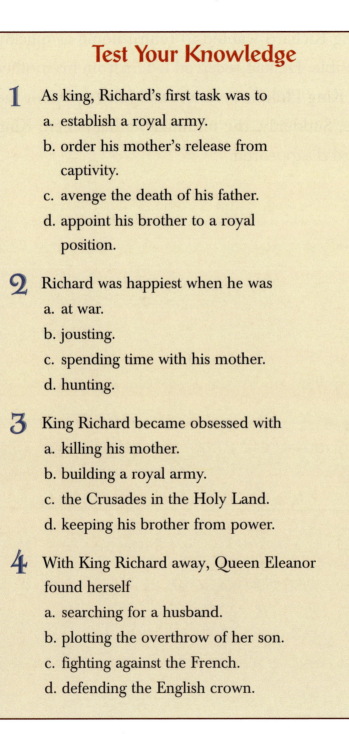

Test Your Knowledge

1 As king, Richard's first task was to

    a. establish a royal army.

    b. order his mother's release from captivity.

    c. avenge the death of his father.

    d. appoint his brother to a royal position.

2 Richard was happiest when he was

    a. at war.

    b. jousting.

    c. spending time with his mother.

    d. hunting.

3 King Richard became obsessed with

    a. killing his mother.

    b. building a royal army.

    c. the Crusades in the Holy Land.

    d. keeping his brother from power.

4 With King Richard away, Queen Eleanor found herself

    a. searching for a husband.

    b. plotting the overthrow of her son.

    c. fighting against the French.

    d. defending the English crown.

5 In what year did the Crusaders win a great victory near Arsuf, Israel?

a. 1191

b. 1419

c. 1219

d. 1119

Protecting the Kingdom

Queen Eleanor frantically worried about her precious son King Richard. Meanwhile, all across England, people lit candles and prayed for the king's safe return. Many people believed that his ship was lost at sea and he had drowned. Queen Berengaria's ship had safely reached land and she was on her way to Rome. No one had seen King Richard's ship since midway through its journey.

Apparently a fierce storm struck at sea. The wild winds blew the royal ship back toward Cyprus. After being blown off course, King Richard hired two Greek pirate ships to escort him through the Adriatic Sea, but another storm shipwrecked the king off the coast of Friuli. With little success at sea, King Richard decided to continue his journey by land. This choice was risky. He was in Austria and, during the siege of Acre, Duke Leopold of Austria had disobeyed King Richard's commands. In punishment, King Richard ordered that the banner of Austria be thrown to the ground. He then stomped it into the mud. The duke swore that King Richard would always be an enemy of Austria.

On his journey, King Richard disguised himself as Hugo, a common merchant, and he avoided capture for quite some time. He was finally arrested on December 21, at a small tavern, dressed as a cook.

Back home, Christmas came and went with still no news from King Richard. On December 28, a messenger arrived with the amazing news that the king was still alive, but he was imprisoned some-where in Austria.

When Queen Eleanor heard the news, she immediately took control of the kingdom. She acted as regent, or ruler, in the king's absence. Queen Eleanor knew that her son was being held captive, but she had no idea where, or what plans the cruel Austrian emperor had for King Richard. She sent abbots to Austria, at once, to search for the king. She wrote a number of angry letters to the pope. She complained that King Richard's arrest violated the Crusaders' truce to God. She also accused the pope of doing nothing to help her son, whom she referred to as the Lord's anointed. In a fit of rage, she even threatened to divide the united Christian kingdom. "The fateful moment is near," she fumed, "when the seamless robe of Christ shall be rent [torn] again." In one letter, she called herself "Eleanor, by the wrath of God, Queen of England."[13]

ANOTHER FIGHT FOR THE THRONE

Once again, King Philip of France and John conspired to take advantage of King Richard's misfortune. King Philip began another attack on Gisors, easily taking control. At long last, King Philip had conquered the Vixen. John called together the barons in Normandy, so they could acknowledge him as his brother's heir. When the barons refused to pay homage to him, John went to Paris. He presented himself as Duke of Normandy, Duke of Aquitaine, and even the king of England. He confirmed the surrender of the Vixen to King Philip. He then divorced his wife and married Alice of France. In anger, he mounted an army of mercenaries, or paid soldiers. His plan was to return to England and take his rightful kingdom by force.

Queen Eleanor reacted shrewdly to John's outlandish behavior. Instead of confronting him, she simply outsmarted him. She called together an army of knights, nobles, guards, and commoners, and dispatched them along the English coast. Most of John's mercenaries were arrested as soon as they landed.

John and a small party still managed to reach England unharmed. He employed another group of mercenaries and took over at Windsor and Wallingford. Eleanor's men besieged John in Windsor and his other holds in England at once.

Even though there was a chance that he might still one day inherit the throne, John stubbornly resisted. The safety of England depended on King Richard's safe and swift return.

At the end of April 1193, an official returned to England with depressing news about King Richard. In order for the king to be set free, a ransom of 100,000 marks, a huge sum for the time, would need to be paid. King Richard would also have to provide military assistance to Germany in an upcoming campaign against Sicily. Apparently, Duke Leopold of Austria had handed Richard over to German Emperor Henry, for 75,000 marks. Emperor Henry, in turn, asked Queen Eleanor for a higher ransom.

Queen Eleanor went about the difficult task of raising the ransom. King Richard had already emptied much of the treasury to finance the Crusade, so the queen issued degrees for new taxes. Unfortunately, Queen Eleanor's new taxes collected much less money than she needed. Many people simply refused to pay. John added to the trouble when he mercilessly collected funds in his own lands, but kept the money for himself. He still hoped his brother would not return.

Meanwhile, new negotiations took place between the German emperor and King Richard. It seemed likely that the king would be released, after all. In July 1193, King Philip of France sent a warning to John, "the devil has been let loose."[14] Terrified, John fled England and joined King Philip in Normandy. Even in exile, John did not give up his plans. He ordered his supporters in England to revolt as soon as they heard that the French had invaded Normandy.

Queen Eleanor again stepped in to save the day. She persuaded the council to seize all of John's land in England. Normandy also remained loyal to the king. By October 1193, Queen Eleanor had raised the necessary 100,000 silver marks—35 tons of precious metal. King Richard was understandably cautious. He did not want anything to go wrong when the ransom money was delievered. He requested that Queen Eleanor personally accompany the silver to Germany. In December, Queen Eleanor set sail with the money. Her fleet was armed with hundreds of soldiers, in the event that pirates tried to capture the valuable cargo.

Queen Eleanor made a smooth crossing over the North Sea. She then traveled by road and again by boat up the Rhine River to Speier. Queen Eleanor was supposed to reunite with her son on January 6, but Emperor Henry decided to postpone King Richard's release. Apparently, France's King Philip and John offered Emperor Henry another 100,000 marks, if he would keep the king imprisoned.

The news broke Queen Eleanor's heart. She had not seen her favorite son for nearly three years, but a surprising twist took place. No doubt, Emperor Henry was tempted by the possibility of more money. In France, John and King Philip were certain the emperor would accept their offer, so they prepared for war. Emperor Henry knew, however, that John and King Philip were not the most reliable business partners. More important, King Richard made many friends during his captivity. His charm won over some powerful allies. The princes of the empire were very impressed by King Richard's success in the Crusade. They rose to the king's defense and pleaded for his release.

The emperor decided it was best to decline John's bribe, but he did want something in return. He demanded that King Richard submit to him as a vassal. While accepting this deal would be humiliating, it was more or less a meaningless request. Queen Eleanor saw this as King Richard's only chance to escape. On her advice, King Richard took off his hat and handed it to the emperor—a sign that he was now a vassal to the emperor of Germany.

At last, King Richard was freed on February 4, 1194. Queen Eleanor and her favorite son were finally reunited. Mother and son cried in each other's arms. In March, mother and son set sail for home.

THE KING RETURNS

At 9:00 A.M., King Richard and Queen Eleanor sailed into the harbor at Sandwich, England. That day, the sun glowed in red brilliance, as if to announce the return of the king. His subjects welcomed him home with loud cheers and tears of joy. The streets were decorated with rich tapestries and evergreen wreaths. One Englishman remembered, "The news of the coming of the king, so long and so desperately awaited, flew faster than the north wind." [15] For his part, King Richard truly appreciated his mother's superb governing while he was away. If it had not been for Queen Eleanor's quick actions, his kingdom would certainly have fallen to rebels.

King Richard did not spend much time celebrating, however. He immediately rode to John's castle in Nottingham. It was time to restore order to the kingdom and deal with his brother's rebel supporters. King Richard and his soldiers besieged Nottingham. When the knights inside the castle saw that it was really King Richard attacking them, they surrendered. John's revolt was quickly crushed. After the fall of Nottingham, King Richard demanded that his brother appear before him within 40 days. If John failed to show, he would give up any right to succeed Richard as king.

One night, a member of the royal court entered King Richard's room. He was obviously too nervous to speak. King Richard guessed that his brother was outside. "I know you have seen my brother," he said. "He is wrong to be afraid—let him come in, without fear. After all, he is my brother." [16] John threw himself down at Richard's feet and begged for forgiveness. The king lovingly pardoned his brother. He blamed John's counselors for misleading him and vowed

King Richard was freed on February 4, 1194, and came home to a rousing celebration. He did not waste time celebrating, however. He immediately set off on horseback to deal with his rebel brother John in Nottingham.

revenge on them. King Richard then ordered that a feast be prepared in honor of his brother.

DEATH OF "THE GREAT ONE"

King Richard spent the rest of his life at war with the French. John was now fighting at his brother's side, with apparent loyalty. King Philip was still determined to bring down King Richard's vast empire. He was, no doubt, one of France's most energetic rulers. He was crafty and greedy. Unlike King Richard, he possessed absolutely no chivalry. He was monstrously unattractive, short, and bulky, with a round, red face and messy hair. Although he was a poor soldier and he had never learned how to ride a horse properly, he was extremely practical. More important, King Philip was not easily discouraged.

By the mid-1190s, King Richard seemed to have almost everything going his way. He had formed strong alliances with kingdoms all around him, including Germany. His wealth seemed limitless, and he led an impressive army. Nevertheless, war between King Richard and King Philip broke out in 1197, and again in 1198. King Richard defeated the French in both battles. In the process, he

Fontevrault

After King Richard's return in 1194, 72-year-old Queen Eleanor retired to her favorite religious house—the abbey in Fontevrault. This convent was located near Chinon, on the borders of Touraine and Anjou. Queen Eleanor did not become a nun, but she found the atmosphere at the abbey very restful.

Throughout Europe, Fontevrault was widely recognized as a center for improving the status of women and defending their rights. This type of house was quite radical in the twelfth century. Battered housewives from all over France fled to the convent, as a safe house, where they could regain their self-respect and confidence.

The mission of Fontevrault, no doubt, appealed to Queen Eleanor. She too had been cast off and mistreated by King Henry II. She was also a devout Christian. For years, Queen Eleanor had made generous donations to the abbey. Eleanor also thought her years of hectic reign were over. Fontevrault was the perfect place for an old woman to prepare her soul for death.

regained the entire Vixen—painfully King Philip's greatest loss.

By 1199, King Philip's hope of expansion looked increasingly bleak. England and the surrounding kingdoms remained under King Richard's grip. Even English rebels had a great deal of respect for their king. Unable to accept defeat, the king of France continued to annoy King Richard.

One day while plowing his field, a peasant, from the kingdom of Limousin in France, dug up a fabulous treasure. The peasant dutifully took the treasure to his lord, who in turn presented it to his overlord. Rumors about the valuable discovery began to spread all over France. Soon, King Richard, too, heard about the treasure. The overlord was King Richard's vassal, so the king demanded that the treasure be handed over to him. The overlord agreed to give King Richard half, but no more.

King Richard was outraged. He desperately needed money. In his war with King Philip, he had hired mercenaries to help him fight. King Richard was running out of money to pay them, and the mercenaries were becoming restless. The king was determined to collect the treasure, which was rightfully

When King Richard was wounded with an arrow, doctors were unable to remove the whole arrow. King Richard died on the evening of April 6, 1199, after a deadly infection set in.

his. He marched his army to the overlord's castle at Châlus and laid siege to it. The castle was guarded by only 50 men, mainly peasants and a few knights.

They foolishly tried to resist. King Richard assumed it would not take long to squash the small rebellion.

On the evening of March 25, the king went out on horseback to see how the fight was coming along. An archer shot King Richard in the shoulder, just below his neck. King Richard, a veteran of the Crusades, was no stranger to wounds, so he calmly returned to his lodge.

When doctors pulled out the arrow, the shaft broke. In order to remove the rest of the arrow, they had to perform an operation. Surgeons managed to get most of the arrow out, but a small fragment of iron remained. Deadly gangrene soon set in, and King Richard realized he was dying. He immediately sent for his mother. On the evening of April 6, 1199, King Richard died in his mother's arms. "The Great One," as Eleanor called him, was gone.

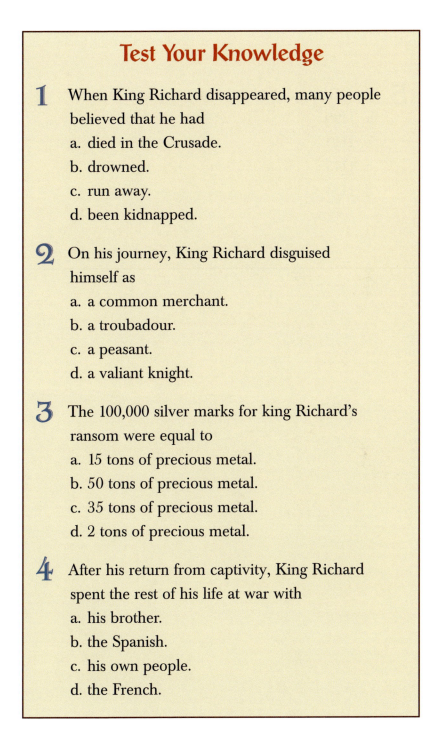

Test Your Knowledge

1 When King Richard disappeared, many people believed that he had
a. died in the Crusade.
b. drowned.
c. run away.
d. been kidnapped.

2 On his journey, King Richard disguised himself as
a. a common merchant.
b. a troubadour.
c. a peasant.
d. a valiant knight.

3 The 100,000 silver marks for king Richard's ransom were equal to
a. 15 tons of precious metal.
b. 50 tons of precious metal.
c. 35 tons of precious metal.
d. 2 tons of precious metal.

4 After his return from captivity, King Richard spent the rest of his life at war with
a. his brother.
b. the Spanish.
c. his own people.
d. the French.

5 King Richard died in what year?
   a. 1199
   b. 1119
   c. 1145
   d. 1154

ANSWERS: 1. b; 2. a; 3. c; 4. d; 5. a

A Fight
for Angevin

The shock of King Richard's death was, without a doubt, the most horrible event in Queen Eleanor's life. She was not, however, inclined to waste time mourning, especially when a kingdom was at stake. The new king of England and lord of the Angevin Empire was John, but he was rivaled by his nephew—12-year-old Arthur, Duke of Brittany, and Geoffrey's son.

By the numbers, Arthur's inheritance came before John's. Arthur was the offspring of King Henry and Queen Eleanor's third son. John was the fourth son of King Henry and Queen Eleanor, placing him further down in line. At one time, King Richard had treated Duke Arthur as his heir. On his deathbed, however, King Richard declared John as his successor. Queen Eleanor showed a preference for John, perhaps so she could retain some power. She also wanted to make sure that the Angevin Empire stayed together.

John was 39 years old when he became king. Not nearly as popular as Richard, he disliked war, was horribly cruel and dishonest, and was known to many as a coward. He did have some talents, though. He could be a shrewd politician and a smooth diplomat. Unfortunately, his bad points outweighed his good qualities.

In no way could John ever replace King Richard, but, he could guarantee power and independence for Queen Eleanor in Poitou and Aquitaine. Queen Eleanor was so masterful that John both trusted and feared her.

Shortly after King Richard's death, Arthur's mother, Constance, rode in to claim Anjou, Maine, and Touraine for her son. King John barely escaped to Normandy. From there, he fled to England. King Philip immediately took advantage of King John's weakened empire. He invaded Normandy and captured Evreux. Yet, Normandy remained faithful to John, and the garrisons held out. They stopped the French army from advancing, and John was crowned king of England. Queen Eleanor, meanwhile, captured the rest of the empire for her son. She toured Poitou and Bordelais and secured her vassals' support. She hired mercenaries to plunder all of occupied Anjou. Constance and Duke Arthur retreated into Maine, where they found safety in the capital city of Le Mans. When King John and his troops attacked Le Mans and completely leveled the city walls, Constance and Duke Arthur again escaped by night. For protection, Duke Arthur went to live with King Philip in Paris. King Philip agreed to raise Duke Arthur. As the newly declared Count of Anjou and Maine, Duke Arthur's loyalty was a valuable asset to King Philip. In reality, however, the entire Angevin Empire was in King John's control.

In order to secure King John's empire from Constance, Queen Eleanor forced herself to do the unthinkable. She went to Tours, France, and knelt down at the feet of her son's most bitter enemy— King Philip. In so doing, she pledged to be a vassal of the king of France. This act blocked Duke Arthur from making any further claims on Poitou or Aquitaine. Eleanor then wrote a deed, willing these lands to her son, but she remained the active ruler for the rest of her life.

For a while, King Philip decided to give up his fight for the Angevin Empire. On May 22, 1200, he and King John signed a treaty. The French king named King John as Count of Anjou and Maine, and declared him to be overlord of Brittany. In return, King John surrendered the Vixen and the country of Evreux. King John also arranged a marriage between his niece and Philip's son—the heir and future king, Louis VIII.

The treaty was a triumph for Queen Eleanor. She had prevailed in a battle of wits with Constance. More important, the marriage of her granddaughter to the young prince would secure the survival of the Angevin Empire.

King John of England pays homage to King Phillip II of France in front of the royal court. The peace treaty between the two kings was a triumph for Queen Eleanor.

THE LUSIGNAN REVOLT

During the summer of 1200, King John traveled throughout Poitou. The dangerous Lusignan family had recently become his allies. King John visited them in Lusignan, where he was warmly welcomed.

During his stay, he was introduced to the beautiful Isabella of Angoulême. She was only about 14 years old and was already betrothed to the head of the Lusignan clan, Count Hugh the Brown.

Although King John was 35, he fell desperately in love with young Isabella. King John sent Count Hugh on a mission to England. With the count out of the way, John took Isabella as his bride. The deceptive marriage was a huge mistake, however. The Lusignan family had many excellent soldiers. They were also rich and powerful, and spread throughout Poitou and Normandy. Count Hugh was determined to have his revenge. In early 1201, the Lusignan family rose up in revolt.

When King John landed in Normandy in May 1201, he had no idea that he was on the verge of war. The Lusignans were still in revolt, but they had been controlled. Castles in Poitou and Normandy had been captured, but the revolt would not die down. The Lusignan family appealed to King Philip, John's overlord. In April 1202, the French king summoned John to appear in court, to answer for his actions. King John failed to show up. In response, on April 28, King Philip declared war.

The king of France struck targets further down the River Seine into northeastern Normandy. He easily captured Aumâle, Boutevant, Gournai, and other important Norman castles. King Philip made it clear that he planned to destroy the Angevin Empire.

At the end of April, King Philip promised his baby daughter to Duke Arthur. Two months later, the young duke pledged homage to King Philip in exchange for Brittany, Anjou, Maine, Touraine, and Poitou. In truth, King Philip had no right to give away these lands. Queen Eleanor's pledge to the French king was still valid. Philip's actions revealed his plan, however, to overthrow King John's kingdoms in France.

In the meantime, King John was preparing a counterattack. He assembled an army in southern Normandy. In July, John received alarming news. Duke Arthur had joined forces with the Lusignan rebels. The young duke learned that his grandmother was on her way to Poitiers. Realizing that Queen Eleanor would be a heavy bargaining chip, he and his army set out to capture her. On her way, Eleanor stopped in Mirebeau. Duke Arthur met up with her there and stormed the town walls.

The feisty old queen fled to a small tower. She fought off her attackers with her few troops and refused to surrender. She finally agreed to bargain with them. Little did Duke Arthur know, she had secretly sent two messengers for help. Instead of storming the tower, Duke Arthur's men waited for Queen Eleanor to surrender.

Meanwhile, one of the queen's messengers reached King John. As soon as he heard about his mother's distress, he rushed to her rescue. Riding day and night, he covered 80 miles in 48 hours. His army reached Mirebeau on the dawn of August 1. It was a hot night, but, without fear, Duke Arthur's men did not bother to sleep in their armor. That morning, a lookout interrupted Geoffrey Lusignan at breakfast to let him know that the king of England was attacking. Lusignan, however, was only concerned about finishing his breakfast.

A terrible battle took place in the narrow streets of Mirebeau. Duke Arthur's troops were trapped and could not escape. King John won an amazing victory—the only major battle he personally commanded. Duke Arthur was captured, however, and thrown into a dungeon.

After his nephew had spent several months in prison, King John visited him. He agreed to set Duke Arthur free and return the duchy of Brittany on two conditions. Duke Arthur had to break his alliance with King Philip and promise his loyalty to John. Even after a long and cruel captivity, Duke Arthur stubbornly refused. Not long after this meeting, Arthur mysteriously vanished.

No one knows exactly what happened to the young duke. Some stories suggest that he was brutally tortured and sent away. Others suggest he fell to his death, trying to escape from a tower. Still another story says that King John murdered his enemy nephew in a drunken rage. According to the story, King John tied a heavy stone to the corpse and dumped it in the River Seine. A fisherman later pulled up the body in his net. Duke Arthur's body was secretly buried.

THE FALL OF THE ANGEVIN EMPIRE

Word of Duke Arthur's disappearance and possible death enraged King Philip. He was already invading Normandy at the time, and his fury helped fuel his fight. By the end of 1203, only a few loyal vassals remained in Normandy. King John seemed to lose touch with reality. He wandered around his camp, muttering that his soldiers should leave him alone. In December, King John left Normandy for England, never to return.

In March 1204, King Philip secured a sure victory in Normandy. The Angevin stronghold in France had fallen. By summer, King John had lost all of Normandy, an inheritance that had been handed down from his great-great-grandfather, William the Conqueror.

The fall of Normandy was the beginning of a string of disasters. Soon after, Anjou also fell. In Poitou, King Philip met with great resistance. Queen Eleanor, who moved from the convent in Fontevrault to Poitiers, had a loyal and skilled commander. Nevertheless, King Philip had no real quarrel with Queen Eleanor. She had already pledged to be his vassal. Eleanor was too old and frail to lead a full-scale war against her invaders, but she did manage to keep her country loyal to her—even to the very end.

On April 1, 1204, Eleanor of Aquitaine died, most likely at Poitiers. She was 82 years old. Her death went almost unnoticed among the chaos, but the Angevin Empire died along with Eleanor of Aquitaine. In a sense, she had created it, so it was only fitting that it should come to an end upon her death. Queen Eleanor probably realized that her unstable and clumsy youngest child would never be able to hold on to such a powerful empire. She must have seen its doom with Richard's death. For almost seven decades, Eleanor of Aquitaine's shrewd genius had held a vast empire together, while still protecting her beloved Aquitaine. She was truly one of the most remarkable women of the Middle Ages.

Test Your Knowledge

1 How old was John when he became king?

    a. 39

    b. 49

    c. 29

    d. 44

2 John was known to many as

    a. a kind man.

    b. a coward.

    c. a good leader.

    d. a religious man.

3 What event was the beginning of a string
of disasters?

    a. The marriage of King John

    b. The death of Eleanor of Aquitaine

    c. The fall of Normandy

    d. The death of King John

4 How old was Eleanor of Aquitaine when
she died?

    a. 56

    b. 82

    c. 62

    d. 78

5 Eleanor of Aquitaine's shrewd genius held a vast empire together for how long?

a. Almost four decades

b. Almost five decades

c. Almost ten decades

d. Almost seven decades

ANSWERS: 1. a; 2. b; 3. c; 4. b; 5. d

1096–1099 First Crusade is fought.

1122 Eleanor of Aquitaine is born in Poitiers, or Belin.

1127 Eleanor's beloved grandfather, Duke William IX, dies.

1137 **April 9** Eleanor's father, William X, dies; Eleanor becomes a duchess and sole heiress to Aquitaine.

July 25 Duchess Eleanor marries Prince Louis of France.

August 1 King Louis VI, or Louis the Fat, dies; Eleanor and Louis VII become king and queen of France.

1143 The new king, Louis VII, invades the town of Vitry, killing 1,300 men, women, and children.

1096–1099
First Crusade
is fought

April 9, 1137 Eleanor's father dies; she becomes Duchess of Aquitaine

July 25, 1137 Duchess Eleanor marries Prince Louis of France

August 1, 1137 King Louis VI dies; Eleanor and Louis VII become king and queen of France

1096

1122
Eleanor of
Aquitaine
is born

1127
Eleanor's
beloved
grandfather
dies

1148
The Second
Crusade ends

March 21, 1152
King Louis and
Queen Eleanor
get a divorce

1158 Queen Eleanor's son Geoffrey is born

1157 Queen Eleanor's favorite son, Richard, is born

1154 Henry and Eleanor are crowned as king and queen of England

May 18, 1152 Queen Eleanor marries Henry II, Duke of Normandy

1147 **June** Queen Eleanor and King Louis set out on the Second Crusade.

1148 Queen Eleanor asks King Louis for an annulment, but King Louis refuses; the Crusaders lose the battle at Damascus, bringing to an end to the Second Crusade.

1151 King Louis and Queen Eleanor return home to Paris.

1152 **March 21** King Louis and Queen Eleanor get a divorce.

May 18 Queen Eleanor marries Henry II, Duke of Normandy without Louis's permission.

1153 Queen Eleanor's first son, William, is born; he dies at age three.

1167 Queen Eleanor's last son, John, is born

July 6, 1189 King Henry II dies in shame after his sons betray him

1173 Queen Eleanor leads her sons in a revolt against their father

September 3, 1189 Richard is crowned king of England; he immediately releases his mother from captivity

1204

1186 Geoffrey dies

1204 Queen Eleanor's Angevin Empire begins to fall; on April 1, Queen Eleanor dies at age 82

September 1174 King Henry makes peace with his sons; Queen Eleanor becomes a prisoner of the king

1154 Henry and Eleanor are crowned as king and queen of England.

1155 Son Henry III is born.

1156 Daughter Matilda is born.

1157 Queen Eleanor's favorite son and heir to Aquitaine, Richard, is born.

1158 Queen Eleanor's son Geoffrey, the most evil of her sons, is born.

1162 Daughter Eleanor is born.

1165 Daughter Joanna is born.

1167 Eleanor's last son, John, the future king, is born.

1173 Eleanor leads her sons in a revolt against their father, King Henry II.

1174 King Henry makes peace with his sons; Eleanor becomes a prisoner of the king for the next 15 years.

1183 Young Henry dies on June 11; Eleanor has a vivid dream in which she sees her son dead.

1186 Geoffrey dies.

1189 **July 6** King Henry II dies in shame after his sons betray him.

September 3 Richard is crowned as king of England; he immediately releases his mother from captivity.

1190 King Richard joins the Third Crusade; while he is away, Queen Eleanor protects his kingdom from his greedy brother John and King Philip of France.

1192 King Richard is arrested and held for ransom in Austria.

1194 **February 4** Thanks to Eleanor's shrewd advice, King Richard is freed from captivity.

March King Richard and Queen Eleanor return to England.

1199 Beloved King Richard dies on April 6; John becomes the new king.

1202 The Lusignan Revolt begins.

1204 Queen Eleanor's Angevin Empire begins to fall; on April 1, Queen Eleanor dies at age 82.

NOTES

CHAPTER 3
Queen Eleanor of France

1. Alison Weir, *Eleanor of Aquitaine: A Life*. New York: Ballantine Books, 1999, p. 30.

CHAPTER 4
Give Us Crosses!

2. Weir, *Eleanor of Aquitaine: A Life*, p. 50.
3. Ibid., p. 55.

CHAPTER 5
A Monk, Not a King

4. Desmond Seward, *Eleanor of Aquitaine: The Mother Queen*. Newton Abbot, England: David & Charles, 1978, p. 57.
5. Ibid., p. 73.
6. Ibid.

CHAPTER 6
Queen Eleanor and Her Sons

7. Seward, *Eleanor of Aquitaine: The Mother Queen*, p. 85.
8. Weir, *Eleanor of Aquitaine: A Life*, p. 181.

CHAPTER 7
Queen Eleanor's Revolt

9. Seward, *Eleanor of Aquitaine: The Mother Queen*, p. 130.
10. Weir, *Eleanor of Aquitaine: A Life*, p. 245.
11. Ibid., p. 246.

CHAPTER 8
The Mother Queen

12. Weir, *Eleanor of Aquitaine: A Life*, p. 248.

CHAPTER 9
Protecting the Kingdom

13. Seward, *Eleanor of Aquitaine: The Mother Queen*, p. 173.
14. Ibid., p. 177.
15. Weir, *Eleanor of Aquitaine: A Life*, p. 297.
16. Seward, *Eleanor of Aquitaine: The Mother Queen*, p. 189.

Kelly, Amy. *Eleanor of Aquitaine and the Four Kings.* Cambridge, MA: J. Margaret Malcolm, 1978.

Lofts, Norah. *Eleanor the Queen: The Story of the Most Famous Woman of the Middle Ages.* Garden City, NY: Doubleday, 1955.

Meade, Marion. *Eleanor of Aquitaine: A Biography.* New York: Hawthorn Books, 1977.

Owen, D.D.R. *Eleanor of Aquitaine: Queen and Legend.* Cambridge, MA: Blackwell, 1993.

Plaidy, Jean. *The Courts of Love.* New York: Putnam, 1988.

Rosenberg, Melrich Vonelm. *Eleanor of Aquitaine, Queen of the Troubadours and the Courts of Love.* Boston: Houghton Mifflin Company, 1937.

Seward, Desmond. *Eleanor of Aquitaine: The Mother Queen.* New York: Barnes & Noble Books, 1993.

Walker, Curtis Howe. *Eleanor of Aquitaine.* Chapel Hill, NC: University of North Carolina Press, 1950.

Weir, Alison. *Eleanor of Aquitaine: A Life.* New York: Ballantine Books, 1999.

Brooks, Polly Schoyer. *Queen Eleanor, Independent Spirit of the Medieval World: A Biography of Eleanor of Aquitaine.* Boston: Houghton Mifflin Company, 1999.

Hilliam, David. *Eleanor of Aquitaine: The Richest Queen in Medieval Europe.* New York: Rosen Publishing Group, 2004.

Seward, Desmond. *Eleanor of Aquitaine: The Mother Queen.* New York: Barnes & Noble Books, 1993.

Weir, Alison. *Eleanor of Aquitaine: A Life.* New York: Ballantine Books, 1999.

Websites

Eleanor of Aquitaine
http://www.byu.edu/ipt/projects/middleages/People/EleanorAquitaine.html

Eleanor of Aquitaine (1122–1204)
http://www.hfac.uh.edu/gbrown/philosophers/leibniz/BritannicaPages/EleanorAquitaine/EleanorAquitaine.html

King's College, Women's History Resources Site
Eleanor of Aquitaine
http://www.kings.edu/womens_history/eleanor.html

Medieval Sourcebook: Peter of Blois: Letter 154, to Queen Eleanor, 1173
http://www.fordham.edu/halsall/source/eleanor.html

The Musical Influence of Eleanor of Aquitaine
http://www.vanderbilt.edu/Blair/Courses/MUSL242/johnspa1.htm

page:

3: © Bibliotheque Nationale/ Lauros/Giraudon/Bridgeman Library

4: © Bibliotheque Nationale/ Bridgeman Library

10: © British Library/ Bridgeman Library

12: © Victoria & Albert Museum/ Bridgeman Library

26: © Vannes Cathedral/ Bridgeman Library

30: © Basilique Saint-Denis/ Lauros/Giraudon /Bridgeman Library

37: © Snark/Art Resource, NY

39: © Snark/Art Resource, NY

42: © Giraudon/Art Resource, NY

55: © St. Peter's, Vatican/ Bridgeman Library

58: © Chetham's Library/ Bridgeman Library

73: © HIP/Art Resource, NY

77: © British Library/Bridgeman Library

95: © HIP/Art Resource, NY

101: © British Library/Bridgeman Library

103: © HIP/Scala/Art Resource, NY

121: © The Stapleton Collection/ Bridgeman Library

125: © Erich Lessing/Art Resource, NY

133: © HIP/Art Resource, NY

Cover: © Erich Lessing/Art Resource, NY

Rachel Koestler-Grack has worked with nonfiction books as an editor and writer since 1999. She lives on a hobby farm near Glencoe, Minnesota. During her career, she has worked extensively on historical topics, including the colonial era, the Civil War era, the Great Depression, and the civil rights movement.

DATE DUE

DEMCO 38-296